SQL
Pocket Guide

Jonathan Gennick

Beijing · Cambridge · Farnham · Köln · Paris · Sebastopol · Taipei · Tokyo

SQL Pocket Guide
by Jonathan Gennick

Copyright © 2004 O'Reilly Media, Inc. All rights reserved.
Printed in the United States of America.

Published by O'Reilly Media, Inc., 1005 Gravenstein Highway North, Sebastopol, CA 95472.

O'Reilly Media, Inc. books may be purchased for educational, business, or sales promotional use. Online editions are also available for most titles (*safari.oreilly.com*). For more information, contact our corporate/institutional sales department: (800) 998-9938 or *corporate@oreilly.com*.

Editor:	Deborah Russell
Production Editor:	Emily Quill
Cover Designer:	Ellie Volckhausen
Interior Designer:	David Futato

Printing History:

March 2004:   First Edition.

0-596-00512-1
[C]   [6/04]

Contents

SQL Pocket Guide

Introduction

This book is an attempt to cram the most useful information about SQL into a pocket-sized guide. It describes SQL data manipulation and transaction control statements—the statements most often used by programmers. It also describes common SQL functions, such as those used for data conversion.

Even though SQL is defined by both ANSI and ISO standards, it is far from being standardized and is implemented with sometimes significant variations between different database platforms. The information in this book takes into account the three widely used, commercial database platforms—Oracle, IBM DB2, and Microsoft SQL Server—as well as the open source platform MySQL. However, not all syntax shown in this book will work on all platforms, and throughout the text I try to point out any platform-specific syntax that I show.

The examples in this book were developed against the following releases:

Oracle Database 10g
IBM DB2 Universal Database Version 8.1
Microsoft SQL Server 2000
MySQL 4.1.1-alpha-standard

Some features described in this book may not be available in earlier releases of these products. If you encounter problems getting a particular feature to work as shown, consult your database-specific documentation to see whether the feature is supported by the database software release you are running.

Organization of This Book

This book begins with the Introduction you are reading now, which describes the overall contents, the sample data used for all the examples in the book, and the typographical conventions. Following the Introduction are sections describing the major functional areas of SQL, including datatype conversion, deleting data, functions, NULLs, selecting data, sorting data, and subqueries.

These topics are organized alphabetically, with section names carefully chosen to correspond to relevant SQL keywords. If you require help writing a join, for example, you should be able to quickly flip through the book and find the section titled "Joining Tables" in between "Inserting Data" and "Literals." Consult the Table of Contents and/or the Index if you don't immediately find what you need.

Within each section, syntax is shown by example rather than by complex language diagrams. I've omitted arcane and uncommonly used syntax for ease of understanding and reference. If you need comprehensive and authoritative syntax, refer to the SQL reference manual for your database platform or to *SQL in a Nutshell* (O'Reilly).

Feedback Needed!

I very much want your feedback on the contents of this book. It's tough to take a large topic such as SQL and cram it into a small pocket guide. While writing this book, I've tried to maintain a focus on the audience I want to reach: programmers who are familiar with SQL and who need to refresh their memories on a point of syntax or usage.

My hope was to include all the many little things (e.g., function parameters) that you tend to forget, and thus have to look up, when writing SQL. Please let me know how well I've succeeded, or not succeeded, in reaching that goal. If you find yourself looking in vain for a piece of information you think belongs in this book, please let me know by sending an email to:

jonathan@gennick.com

I'll take all comments that I receive into consideration when I work on the second edition.

Conventions

The following typographical conventions are used in this book:

UPPERCASE
Indicates a SQL keyword

lowercase
Indicates a user-defined item, such as a table name or column name, in a SQL statement

Italic
Indicates emphasis or the introduction of a new technical term

`Constant width`
Used for code examples, and for in-text references to table names, column names, expressions, and so forth

`Constant width bold`
Indicates user input in code examples showing both input and output

`Constant width italic`
Indicates an element of syntax you need to supply when executing a statement or a function

[ ] Used in syntax descriptions to denote optional elements

{ } Used in syntax descriptions to denote a required choice

| Used in syntax descriptions to separate choices

Acknowledgments

My heartiest thanks to the following people for their support, encouragement, and assistance: Debby Russell, Donna, Jenny, and Jeff Gennick, Andrew and Aaron Sears, Ted Rexstrew, Fred Zemke, Jim Melton, John Haydu, Ari Mozes, Tugrul Bingol, Arup Nanda, Vladimir Begun, Doug Doole, Peter Linsley, Tanel Poder, Grant Allen, K. Gopalakrishnan, April Wells, Brand Hunt, Chris Eaton, Dias Costa, John Blake, Nuno Souto, Stephen Lee, Tanel Poder, Don Bales, and Chris Kempster.

Example Data

All example SQL statements in this book execute against a set of tables and data that you can download from this book's catalog page: *http://www.oreilly.com/catalog/sqlpr*. The tables are described in the following sections. To see the data, you'll need to download the scripts. Each script creates tables and data for each platform.

The attraction example

A set of three tables contains information on tourist attractions in Michigan's Upper Peninsula. Figure 1 illustrates the relationships between the tables.

The CD example

Three tables hold information about musical artists, their albums, and the songs on those albums. Figure 2 shows how the tables relate.

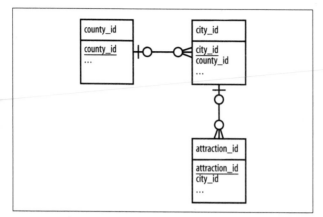

Figure 1. Relationships between the tourist attraction tables

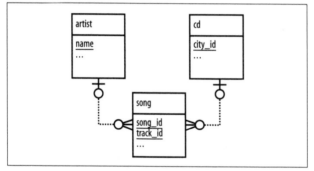

Figure 2. Relationships between the CD tables

The exposure example

Two tables track employee exposure to chemicals over time and illustrate some issues involving temporal data. Figure 3 shows the table relationships.

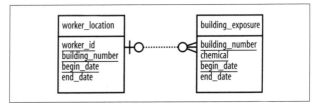

Figure 3. Relationships between the exposure tables

The bill-of-materials example

Recursive query examples are illustrated using the bill-of-materials scenario shown in Figure 4.

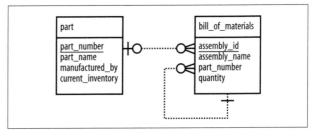

Figure 4. Relationships between the bill-of-materials tables

The pivot table

Some SQL examples in this book use a *pivot table*, which is nothing more than a single-column table containing sequentially numbered rows, in this case 1000 rows. Example 1 shows how to create the pivot table in an Oracle database.

Example 1. SQL statement to create the pivot table

```
CREATE TABLE pivot (
    x NUMBER
    );
```

CASE Expressions

CASE expressions let you implement if-then-else functionality in your SQL statements. You can use them to transform coded values into something that's human-readable, to execute functions conditionally, and much more.

TIP

Oracle's DECODE function, briefly described in the section on "NULLs," can be used to implement if-then logic in SQL statements. Use CASE where possible, though, because CASE is ANSI/ISO-standard.

Simple CASE Expressions

Simple CASE expressions let you correlate a list of values to a list of alternatives:

```
CASE value0
    WHEN value1 THEN return1
    [WHEN value2 THEN return2
    ...]
    [ELSE return_otherwise]
END
```

For example:

```
SELECT attraction_name,
       CASE government_owned
           WHEN 'Y' THEN 'Public'
           WHEN 'N' Then 'Private'
           ELSE 'Bad code'
       END
FROM attraction;
```

```
ATTRACTION_NAME                       CASEGOVE
------------------------------------- --------
Pictured Rocks                        Public
Valley Spur                           Public
Shipwreck Tours                       Private
```

Simple CASE expressions are useful when you can directly link an input value to a WHEN clause via an equality condition.

Note that if no WHEN clause is a match, and no ELSE is specified, the expression returns NULL.

Searched CASE Expressions

Searched CASE expressions let you associate a list of alternative return values with a list of TRUE/FALSE conditions. The first WHEN clause with a condition evaluating to TRUE is the one that is executed:

```
CASE
    WHEN condition1 THEN return1
    [WHEN condition2 THEN return2
    ...]
    [ELSE return_otherwise]
END
```

For example:

```
SELECT COUNT(*), CASE
    WHEN c.city_name IN ('Munising', 'Germfask')
        THEN 'Munising area'
    WHEN c.city_name IN ('Marquette', 'Ishpeming')
        THEN 'Marquette area'
    WHEN c.city_name IN ('Copper Harbor',
                         'Hancock', 'L''Anse')
        THEN 'Keweenaw area'
    ELSE 'Other areas'
    END
FROM city c INNER JOIN attraction a
    ON c.city_id = a.city_id
GROUP BY CASE
    WHEN c.city_name IN ('Munising', 'Germfask')
        THEN 'Munising area'
    WHEN c.city_name IN ('Marquette', 'Ishpeming')
        THEN 'Marquette area'
    WHEN c.city_name IN ('Copper Harbor',
                         'Hancock', 'L''Anse')
        THEN 'Keweenaw area'
    ELSE 'Other areas'
    END;
```

```
COUNT(*) CASEWHENC.CITY
---------- ---------------
         5 Keweenaw area
         5 Marquette area
         4 Munising area
         6 Other areas
```

As with simple CASE expressions, if no condition is TRUE, and no ELSE is specified, then NULL is returned. If multiple conditions are TRUE, only the first such condition counts.

Datatype Conversion

Conversion from one datatype to another—for example, from string to numeric or from numeric to datetime—can be done either explicitly or implicitly. Implicit type conversion can be risky. For example, Oracle will deal with the type mismatch between city_id and the string literal '1' in the following statement:

```
SELECT * FROM city
WHERE city_id = '1';
```

But in the statement shown here, are city_id values converted to text, or is '1' converted to a number? Do you know for sure? What's the impact on index usage? Are the answers the same across database brands?

The following sections describe datatype conversions for each database platform—Oracle, DB2, SQL Server, and MySQL. First, though, let's look at the ANSI/ISO standard CAST and EXTRACT functions.

ANSI/ISO CAST Function

The ANSI/ISO standard provides the CAST function, giving you explicit control over type conversion. For example, to ensure that '1' is converted to a number instead of all the city_id values being converted to strings, you could write:

```
SELECT * FROM city
WHERE city_id = CAST('1' AS NUMBER);
```

This example uses the Oracle datatype NUMBER. The general format for the CAST function is:

```
CAST(value AS datatype)
```

If *value* is a string, it needs to conform to your database's default text representation of the target datatype. For example, the default DATE format in Oracle is usually DD-MON-RR, so the following cast will work:

```
CAST('15-Nov-1961' AS DATE)
```

But if your date is in any other format, the CAST will fail:

```
CAST('11-15-1961' AS DATE)
```

CAST can also be used to convert *to* a text value:

```
SELECT CAST(city_id AS VARCHAR2(10)), city_name
FROM city;
```

When converting from text to numeric or date types, CAST offers little flexibility in dealing with different input data formats. All of the databases described in this book offer much more robust datatype conversion functionality, which I describe in subsequent sections.

NOTE

MySQL seems particularly restrictive about the target datatype of a CAST, allowing you to CAST only to the following: BINARY, DATE, DATETIME, SIGNED INTEGER, TIME, and UNSIGNED INTEGER.

ANSI/ISO EXTRACT Function

ANSI/ISO provides for the following function to extract elements from a datetime value:

```
EXTRACT(element_keyword FROM datetime)

element_keyword ::= {SECOND|MINUTE|HOUR
                     |DAY|MONTH|YEAR}
```

EXTRACT always returns a numeric value. The following MySQL example uses EXTRACT to return the current day of the month:

```
SELECT EXTRACT(DAY FROM CURRENT_DATE);
```

    4

Oracle and MySQL support the EXTRACT function. Oracle supports the following additional elements: TIMEZONE_HOUR, TIMEZONE_MINUTE, TIMEZONE_REGION, and TIMEZONE_ABBR. The latter two Oracle elements are exceptions to the rule, and return string values.

Datetime Conversions (Oracle)

You can convert to and from datetime types in Oracle using the following functions:

```
TO_CHAR({datetime|interval}, format)
TO_DATE(string, format)
TO_TIMESTAMP(string, format)
TO_TIMESTAMP_TZ(string, format)
TO_DSINTERVAL('D HH:MI:SS')
TO_YMINTERVAL('Y-M')
```

When converting a datetime value from its textual representation, use a *format* string to describe the input format. When converting to a textual representation, use the *format* string to describe your desired output format. See Table 1 for descriptions of *format* string elements.

Table 1. Oracle's date format elements

Element	Description
AM or PM A.M. or P.M.	Meridian indicator, with or without periods.
BC or AD B.C. or A.D.	B.C. or A.D. indicator, with or without periods.
CC	Century. Output-only.
D	Day in the week. NLS_TERRITORY determines which day is day 1.

Table 1. Oracle's date format elements (continued)

Element	Description
DAY, Day, or day	Name of day. Case follows format.
DD	Day in the month.
DDD	Day in the year.
DL	Long date format. Output-only. Combines only with TS.
DS	Short date format. Output-only. Combines only with TS.
DY, Dy, or dy	Abbreviated name of day. Case follows format.
E	Abbreviated era name for Japanese Imperial, ROC Official, and Thai Buddha calendars. Input-only.
EE	Full era name.
FF, FF1...FF9	Fractional seconds. Only for TIMESTAMP values. Always use two F's. FF1...FF9 work in Oracle Database 10*g* and higher.
FM	Toggles suppression of blanks in output from conversion.
FX	Requires exact pattern matching between input data and format model.
HH or HH12	Hour in the day, from 1–12. HH12 is output-only.
HH24	Hour in the day, from 0–23.
IW	ISO week in the year. Output-only.
IYY or IY or I	Last three, two, or one digits of ISO standard year. Output-only.
IYYY	ISO standard year. Output-only.
J	Julian date. January 1, 4712 B.C. is day 1.
MI	Minutes.
MM	Month number.
MON, Mon, or mon	Abbreviated name of month. Case follows format.
MONTH, Month, or month	Name of month. Case follows format.
Q	Quarter of year. Output-only.
RM	Roman numeral month number.
RR	Last two digits of year. Sliding window for century: 00–49/50–99.
RRRR	Four-digit year; also accepts two digits on input. Sliding window just like RR.

Table 1. Oracle's date format elements (continued)

Element	Description
SCC	Century. B.C. dates negative. Output-only.
SP	Suffix that converts a number to its spelled format.
SPTH	Suffix that converts a number to its spelled and ordinal format.
SS	Seconds.
SSSSS	Seconds since midnight.
SYEAR, SYear, syear	Year in words. B.C. dates negative. Case follows format. Output-only.
SYYYY	Four-digit year. B.C. dates negative.
TH	Suffix that converts a number to ordinal format.
TS	Short time format. Output-only. Combine only with DL or DS.
TZD	Abbreviated time zone name. Input-only.
TZH	Time zone hour displacement from UTC (Universal Coordinated Time).
TZM	Time zone minute displacement from UTC.
TZR	Time zone region.
W	Week in the month, from 1 through 5. Week 1 starts on the first day of the month and ends on the seventh. Output-only.
WW	Week in the year, from 1 through 53. Output-only.
X	Local radix character used to denote the decimal point. This is a period in American English.
Y,YYY	Four-digit year with comma.
YEAR, Year, year	Year in words. Case follows format. Output-only.
YYY or YY or Y	Last three, two, or one digits of year.
YYYY	Four-digit year.

The TO_DSINTERVAL and TO_YMINTERVAL functions, which are used to convert to interval types, are exceptions to the rule in that they support only one input format each, as shown in the earlier list.

In all cases, the *format* string is optional. You can omit it when your input value conforms to the default format specified by:

- NLS_DATE_FORMAT for dates
- NLS_TIMESTAMP_FORMAT for timestamps
- NLS_TIMESTAMP_TZ_FORMAT for timestamps with time zones

You can query the NLS_SESSION_PARAMETERS view to check your NLS settings.

Following are some example conversions:

```
SELECT chemical FROM building_exposure
WHERE building_number = 2
AND begin_date
    >= TO_DATE('Apr 27, 1998','Mon dd, yyyy');

SELECT chemical FROM building_exposure
WHERE building_number = 2
AND begin_date
    >= TO_DATE('27-Apr-1998 8:00 AM',
               'dd-mon-yyyy hh:mi am');

SELECT chemical,
       TO_CHAR(begin_date,
               'Month dd, yyyy hh:mi PM')
FROM building_exposure
WHERE building_number = 2;
```

All but the interval conversion functions take a third (optional) string argument named *nlsparam* with the following content:

```
NLS_DATE_LANGUAGE=language
```

With this, you can specify the date language used for month names and so forth. See Appendix A of the *Oracle Database Globalization Support Guide* for a list of valid languages.

TO_YMINTERVAL takes no *nlsparam* parameter. TO_DSINTERVAL takes one in the following form (but appears to ignore it), where *d* specifies a decimal separator and *g* specifies a group separator:

```
NLS_NUMERIC_CHARACTERS=dg
```

Finally, Oracle provides the following two functions to generate interval values from numeric values:

NUMTODSINTERVAL(*number, unit*)

Converts the input number to an INTERVAL DAY TO SECOND value. The unit parameter may be 'DAY', 'HOUR', 'MINUTE', or 'SECOND'.

NUMTOYMINTERVAL(*number, unit*)

Converts the input number to an INTERVAL YEAR TO MONTH value. The unit parameter may be either 'YEAR' or 'MONTH'.

Numeric Conversions (Oracle)

Use the following functions in Oracle to convert to and from the supported numeric types:

```
TO_NUMBER(string, format)
TO_CHAR(number, format)

TO_BINARY_DOUBLE(number)
TO_BINARY_FLOAT(number)
TO_NUMBER(number)

TO_BINARY_DOUBLE(string, format)
TO_BINARY_FLOAT(string, format)
```

Table 2 lists the numeric format elements recognized by these functions.

Table 2. Oracle's numeric format elements

Element	Description
$	Prefix: dollar sign ($).
, (comma)	Specifies location of comma as group separator. Consider using G instead.

Table 2. Oracle's numeric format elements (continued)

Element	Description
. (period)	Specifies location of period as decimal point. Consider using D instead.
0	Significant digit. Leading zeros display as zeros.
9	Significant digit. Leading zeros display as blanks.
B	Prefix: returns a zero value as blanks.
C	Specifies location of ISO currency symbol.
D	Specifies location of decimal point.
EEEE	Suffix: use scientific notation.
FM	Prefix: removes leading/trailing blanks.
G	Specifies location of group separator.
L	Specifies location of local currency symbol.
MI	Suffix: trailing minus (−) sign.
PR	Suffix: angle brackets (< and >) around negative values.
RN or rn	Roman numerals, upper- or lowercase. Output-only.
S	Prefix: leading plus (+) or minus (−) sign.
TM, TM9, TME	Prefix: use minimum number of characters (text-minimum). Output-only. TM9 gives decimal notation. TME gives scientific notation.
U	Specifies location of Euro symbol (€).
V	Multiplies the number to the left of the V in the format model by 10 raised to the *n*th power, where *n* is the number of 9s found after the V in the format model.
X	Use hexadecimal notation. Output-only. Precede with 0s for leading zeros. Precede with FM to trim leading/trailing spaces.

Use TO_NUMBER and TO_CHAR (the only two functions available prior to Oracle Database 10*g*) to convert between NUMBER and VARCHAR2:

```
SET SERVEROUTPUT ON
DECLARE
    x NUMBER;
    y NUMBER;
    z NUMBER;
```

```
BEGIN
   x := TO_NUMBER('12.34','999D99');
   y := TO_NUMBER('1.2345E+2','9.9999EEEE');
   z := TO_NUMBER('9876543.21');

   DBMS_OUTPUT.PUT_LINE(
      TO_CHAR(x,'099.99'));
   DBMS_OUTPUT.PUT_LINE(
      TO_CHAR(y,'9.9EEEE'));
   DBMS_OUTPUT.PUT_LINE(
      TO_CHAR(z,'$999G999G999D99'));
   DBMS_OUTPUT.PUT_LINE(
      TO_CHAR(1961,'RN'));
END;
/

012.34
1.2E+02
$9,876,543.21
MCMLXI
```

Oracle Database 10g adds support for the 32- and 64-bit IEEE 754 floating-point types BINARY_FLOAT and BINARY_DOUBLE. New conversion functions support these types:

```
SELECT TO_BINARY_FLOAT('12.34','999D99')
FROM dual;

SELECT TO_BINARY_DOUBLE('1.2345E+2','9.9999EEEE')
FROM dual;
```

You can also use the conversion functions to convert freely between the different numeric types:

```
DECLARE
   x NUMBER := 1;
   y BINARY_FLOAT;
   z BINARY_DOUBLE;
BEGIN
   y := TO_BINARY_FLOAT(x);
   z := TO_BINARY_DOUBLE(y);
   x := TO_NUMBER(z);
   DBMS_OUTPUT.PUT_LINE(x);
END;
/
```

Miscellaneous Conversions (Oracle)

To convert LOB or text data to CLOB or NCLOB respectively, specify:

```
TO_CLOB({lob|char})
TO_NCLOB({lob|char})
```

To convert to the database or national character sets respectively, specify:

```
TO_CHAR({nchar|clob|nclob})
TO_NCHAR({char|clob|nclob})
```

To convert between single-byte characters and their multi-byte equivalents, specify:

```
TO_MULTI_BYTE(string)
TO_SINGLE_BYTE(string)
```

Use TO_LOB as follows to convert LONG and LONG RAW values to BLOB and CLOB respectively:

```
INSERT INTO target_table (blob_column, clob_column)
    SELECT TO_LOB(long_raw), TO_LOB(long)
    FROM source_table;
```

You can use TO_LOB in this manner only in the SELECT list of a subquery feeding an INSERT statement.

Datetime Conversions (DB2)

You can use the following functions to convert to and from dates, times, and timestamps. In the syntax, *datetime* can be a date, time, or timestamp; *date* must be either a date or a timestamp; *time* must be either a time or a timestamp; and *timestamp* must be a timestamp.

```
BIGINT(datetime)
CHAR(datetime, [ISO|USA|EUR|JIS|LOCAL])
DATE(date)
DATE(integer)
DATE('yyyyddd')
DAY(date)
DAYNAME(date)
DAYOFWEEK(date)
```

```
DAYOFWEEK_ISO(date)
DAYOFYEAR(date)
DAYS(date)
DECIMAL(datetime[,scale[,precision]])
HOUR(time)
JULIAN_DAY(date)
MICROSECOND(timestamp)
MIDNIGHT_SECONDS(time)
MINUTE(time)
MONTH(date)
MONTHNAME(date)
QUARTER(date)
SECOND(time)
TIME(time)
TIMESTAMP(timestamp)
TIMESTAMP(date, time)
TIMESTAMP('yyyymmddhhmiss')
TIMESTAMP_FORMAT(string, C)
TIMESTAMP_ISO(datetime)
TO_CHAR(string, 'YYYY-MM-DD HH24:MI:SS')
TO_DATE(string, 'YYYY-MM-DD HH24:MI:SS')
VARCHAR(datetime)
VARCHAR_FORMAT(timestamp, 'YYYY-MM-DD HH24:MI:SS')
WEEK(date)
WEEK_ISO(date)
YEAR(date)
```

The following example combines the use of several functions that extract various elements of a date to produce a formatted result:

```
SELECT worker_id, building_number,
       MONTHNAME(begin_date) || ' '
       || RTRIM(CHAR(DAY(begin_date))) || ', '
       || RTRIM(CHAR(YEAR(begin_date))) begin_date
FROM worker_location;

WORKER_ID BUILDING_NUMBER BEGIN_DATE
--------- --------------- -------------------------
        1               1 November 15, 2000
        1               2 January 2, 2002
        2               1 December 26, 1995
        2               2 July 1, 1997
        2               3 December 31, 2001
```

Functions requiring date, time, or timestamp arguments also accept character strings that can be implicitly converted into values of those types. For example:

```
SELECT DATE('2003-11-7') ,
       TIME('21:25:00'),
       TIMESTAMP('2003-11-7 21:25:00.00')
FROM pivot
WHERE x =1;

1          2        3
---------- -------- --------------------------
11/07/2003 21:25:00 2003-11-07-21.25.00.000000
```

Using the CHAR function, you can format dates, times, and timestamps in different ways depending on the second argument:

```
SELECT CHAR(current_date, ISO),
       CHAR(current_date, LOCAL),
       CHAR(current_date, USA)
FROM pivot
WHERE x=1;

1          2          3
---------- ---------- ----------
2003-11-06 11-06-2003 11/06/2003
```

The DATE function can convert an integer to a date. Valid integers range from 1 to 3,652,059, where 1 represents 1-Jan-0001. The DAYS function can convert in the reverse direction:

```
SELECT DATE(716194), DAYS('1961-11-15')
FROM pivot
WHERE x=1;

1          2
---------- -----------
11/15/1961      716194
```

Use the DECIMAL function to return dates, times, and timestamps as decimal values taking the forms *yyyymmdd*, *hhmmss*, and *yyyymmddhhmmss.nnnnnnn* respectively:

```
SELECT DECIMAL(current_date),
       DECIMAL(current_time),
```

```
        DECIMAL(current_timestamp)
FROM pivot
WHERE x=1;

1              2         3
----------     --------  ----------------------
20031106.      213653.   20031106213653.088001
```

The BIGINT function returns the same results as DECIMAL
except that the return datatype is BIGINT.

The JULIAN_DAY function returns the number of days since
1-Jan-4713 B.C. (the same as 1-Jan in the astronomical year
−4712), counting that date as day 0. There is no function to
convert in the reverse direction.

Numeric Conversions (DB2)

Use the following functions to convert between different
numeric types or between numeric and text types. See
"Datetime Conversions (DB2)" for information on converting between dates and numbers. In the syntax, *numeric* can
be any numeric type or expression; *character* can be any
fixed- or variable-length character type or expression;
integer can be any integer type or expression; and *decimal*
can be any decimal type or expression.

```
BIGINT(numeric)
BIGINT(character)
CHAR(integer)
CHAR(decimal [,decimal_character])
CHAR(floating [,decimal_character])
DECIMAL(numeric [,precision[,scale]])
DECIMAL(character [,precision[,scale
                   [,decimal_character]]])
DOUBLE(numeric)
DOUBLE(character)
DOUBLE_PRECISION(numeric)
FLOAT(numeric)
REAL(numeric)
SMALLINT(numeric)
SMALLINT(character)
```

Each function converts its argument to the type indicated by the function name. Thus, BIGINT converts values from other numeric types to the BIGINT type, or it converts the character string representation of a number to a BIGINT.

The following example shows CHAR and DECIMAL being used to convert back and forth between numbers and strings:

```
SELECT CHAR(100.12345),
       CHAR(DECIMAL('100.12345',5,2))
FROM pivot
WHERE x=1;

1          2
---------- -------
100.12345  100.12
```

DECIMAL's default scale is zero when converting from a character string. To preserve digits to the right of the decimal point in that situation, you must specify a scale, which forces you to first specify a precision. No rounding occurs. To round a value being converted, first specify a precision and scale sufficient to hold the raw value, and then apply the ROUND function:

```
SELECT DECIMAL('10.999',4,2), DECIMAL('10.999',4),
       ROUND(DECIMAL('10.999',5,3),2)
FROM pivot
WHERE x=1;

1      2      3
------ ------ --------
 10.99 10.    11.000
```

You can use the optional *decimal_character* parameter to specify the character to use for the decimal point:

```
SELECT DECIMAL('10/95',4,2,'/'), CHAR(10.95,'/')
FROM pivot
WHERE x=1;

1      2
------ ------
 10.95 10/95
```

The following example converts a value from a character string to a DOUBLE, and then to a BIGINT:

```
SELECT DOUBLE('10.95'), BIGINT(DOUBLE('10.95'))
FROM pivot
WHERE x=1;
```

1	2
+1.09500000000000E+001	10

When converting to an integer type, any decimal portion is truncated.

Miscellaneous Conversions (DB2)

DB2 supports the following miscellaneous conversion functions:

```
BLOB(character [,length])
CHAR(character [,length])
CLOB(character [,length])
DBCLOB(graphic [,length])
LONG_VARCHAR(character)
VARCHAR(character [,length])
VARCHAR(graphic [,length])
```

Datetime Conversions (SQL Server)

In SQL Server, you have a few options for datetime conversions. You can use the CONVERT function to convert datetime values to strings, but CONVERT supports a limited number of output styles. If you need more flexibility, you can use the DATENAME and DATEPART functions. SQL Server also supports functions to set the datetime format and to extract year, month, and day values from dates.

CAST and SET DATEFORMAT (SQL Server)

SQL Server supports the ANSI/ISO CAST function, and also allows you to specify a datetime format using the SET DATE-FORMAT command:

```
SET DATEFORMAT mdy
SELECT CAST('1/12/2004' AS datetime)
```

    2004-01-12 00:00:00.000

```
SET DATEFORMAT dmy
SELECT CAST('1/12/2004' AS datetime)
```

    2004-12-01 00:00:00.000

For dates in unambiguous formats, you may not need to worry about the DATEFORMAT setting:

```
SET DATEFORMAT dmy
SELECT CAST('12-Jan-2004' AS datetime)
```

    2004-01-12 00:00:00.000

When using SET DATEFORMAT, you can specify any of the following arguments: mdy, dmy, ymd, myd, and dym.

CONVERT (SQL Server)

You can use the CONVERT function for general datetime conversions:

```
CONVERT(datatype[(length)], expression[, style])
```

The optional *style* argument allows you to specify the target and source formats for datetime values, depending on whether you are converting to or from a character string. Table 3 lists the supported styles.

Table 3. SQL Server datetime styles

Style	Description
0, 100	Default: mon dd yyyy hh:miAM (or PM)
101[a]	USA: mm/dd/yyyy
102[a]	ANSI: yyyy.mm.dd
103[a]	British/French: dd/mm/yyyy
104[a]	German: dd.mm.yyyy
105[a]	Italian: dd-mm-yyyy
106[a]	dd mon yyyy
107[a]	mon dd, yyyy
108[a]	hh:mm:ss

Table 3. SQL Server datetime styles (continued)

Style	Description
9, 109	Default with milliseconds: mon dd yyyy hh:mi:ss:mmmAM (or PM)
110[a]	USA: mm-dd-yyyy
111[a]	Japan: yyyy/mm/dd
112[a]	ISO: yyyymmdd
13, 113	Europe default with milliseconds and 24-hour clock: dd mon yyyy hh:mm:ss:mmm
114[a]	hh:mi:ss:mmm with a 24-hour clock
20, 120	ODBC canonical, 24-hour clock: yyyy-mm-dd hh:mi:ss
21, 121	ODBC canonical with milliseconds, 24-hour clock: yyyy-mm-dd hh:mi:ss.mmm
126	ISO8601, no spaces: yyyy-mm-yyThh:mm:ss:mmm
130	Kuwaiti: dd mon yyyy hh:mi:ss:mmmAM
131	Kuwaiti: dd/mm/yyyy hh:mi:ss:mmmAM

[a] Subtract 100 to get a two-digit year.

The following examples demonstrate conversion to and from a date using CONVERT:

```
SELECT CONVERT(
        VARCHAR,
        CONVERT(DATETIME, '15-Nov-1961', 106), 106)

-------------------------------
15 Nov 1961

SELECT CONVERT(
        VARCHAR,
        CONVERT(DATETIME,
                'Nov 11 2003 07:25:00:000PM', 9), 126)

-------------------------------
2003-11-11T19:25:00
```

Use the *length* argument if you want to specify the length of the resulting character string type:

```
SELECT CONVERT(
        VARCHAR(11),
        CONVERT(DATETIME, '15-Nov-1961', 106), 106)

-----------
15 Nov 1961
```

Subtract 100 from most style numbers to support two-digit years:

```
SELECT CONVERT(DATETIME, '1/1/50', 1)

---------------------------------------
1950-01-01 00:00:00.000

SELECT CONVERT(DATETIME, '49.1.1', 2)

---------------------------------------
2049-01-01 00:00:00.000
```

When working with two-digit years, SQL Server uses the year 2049 as a cutoff. Years 50–99 are interpreted as 1950–1999. Years 00–49 are treated as 2000–2049. You can see this behavior in the preceding example. Be aware that your DBA can change the cutoff value using the two digit year cutoff configuration option.

DATENAME and DATEPART (SQL Server)

Use the DATENAME and DATEPART functions to extract specific elements from datetime values:

```
DATENAME(datepart, datetime)
DATEPART(datepart, datetime)
```

The difference between the two functions is that DATE-NAME returns a textual representation of a datetime element, and DATEPART returns a numeric representation. For example:

```
SELECT DATENAME(month, GETDATE()),
       DATEPART(month, GETDATE())

-----------  ---
January        1
```

Some elements, such as *year* and *day*, are represented as numbers no matter what. However, the two functions give you the choice of getting back a string or an actual numeric value. Both of the following function calls return the year, but DATENAME returns the string '2004', whereas DATEPART returns the number 2004:

```
SELECT DATENAME(year, GETDATE()),
       DATEPART(year, GETDATE())
```

SQL Server supports the following *datepart* keywords: year, yy, yyyy, quarter, qq, q, month, mm, m, dayofyear, dy, y, day, dd, d, week, wk, ww, hour, hh, minute, mi, n, second, ss, s, millisecond, ms.

DAY, MONTH, and YEAR (SQL Server)

SQL Server also supports a few functions to extract specific values from dates:

```
DAY(datetime)
MONTH(datetime)
YEAR(datetime)
```

For example:

```
SELECT DAY(CURRENT_TIMESTAMP),
       MONTH(CURRENT_TIMESTAMP),
       YEAR(CURRENT_TIMESTAMP)
```

```
----------- ----------- -----------
11          11          2003
```

Think of these functions as optimized versions of DATEPART. They're an easy way to return numeric day, month, and year values from a datetime value.

Numeric Conversions (SQL Server)

Use the CONVERT function for conversions to and from numeric values:

```
CONVERT(datatype[(length)], expression[, style])
```

Table 4 lists styles for converting FLOAT and REAL values to character strings. Table 5 lists styles for converting MONEY and SMALLMONEY values to character strings.

Table 4. SQL Server floating-point styles

Style	Description
0	Default style, 0–6 digits, scientific notation only when necessary
1	Eight digits + scientific notation
2	16 digits + scientific notation

Table 5. SQL Server money styles

Style	Description
0	Money default, no commas, two decimal digits
1	Commas every three digits, two decimal digits
2	No commas, four decimal digits

The following examples show conversions to and from various numeric types:

```
SELECT CONVERT(VARCHAR, CAST(1.234567 AS REAL))

-------------------------------
1.23457

SELECT CONVERT(VARCHAR, CAST(1.234567 AS REAL), 0)

-------------------------------
1.23457

SELECT CONVERT(VARCHAR,
              CONVERT(FLOAT, '1.234567'), 1)

-------------------------------
1.2345670e+000
```

Following is a sample monetary type conversion:

```
SELECT CONVERT(
        VARCHAR,
        CONVERT(MONEY, '20999.95'), 1)
```

```
--------------------------------
20,999.95
```

Miscellaneous Conversions (SQL Server)

For conversions other than those described in the preceding two sections, use either the CONVERT function or the ANSI-standard CAST expression.

Following is an example of using CONVERT to convert DECIMAL values to BIGINTs:

```
SELECT CONVERT(BIGINT, CAST(14 AS DECIMAL))
```

```
--------------------
14
```

For examples of CAST, see the earlier section "ANSI/ISO CAST Function."

Datetime Conversions (MySQL)

MySQL implements the datetime conversion functions categorized in the following subsections. MySQL supports the ANSI/ISO EXTRACT function described earlier, and supports CASTing strings to the datetime types.

Returning date and time elements (MySQL)

MySQL supports the following functions to return specific date and time elements:

```
DAYOFWEEK(date)
WEEKDAY(date)
DAYOFMONTH(date)
DAYOFYEAR(date)
MONTH(date)
DAYNAME(date)
MONTHNAME(date)
QUARTER(date)
WEEK(date)
WEEK(date, first)
YEAR(date)
YEARWEEK(date)
```

```
YEARWEEK(date,first)
HOUR(time)
MINUTE(time)
SECOND(time)
```

For example, to return the current date in dd-Month-yyyy format, specify:

```
SELECT CONCAT(DAYOFMONTH(CURRENT_DATE), '-',
              MONTHNAME(CURRENT_DATE), '-',
              YEAR(CURRENT_DATE));
```

2-January-2004

For functions taking a *first* argument, you can use this argument to specify whether weeks begin on Sunday (*first* = 0) or Monday (*first* = 1).

TO_DAYS and FROM_DAYS (MySQL)

Use TO_DAYS to convert a date into the number of days since the beginning of the Christian calendar (1-Jan-0001 is considered day 1):

```
SELECT TO_DAYS(CURRENT_DATE);
```

731947

Use FROM_DAYS to convert in the reverse direction:

```
SELECT FROM_DAYS(731947);
```

2004-01-02

One use for these functions is to find the number of days between two dates:

```
SELECT TO_DAYS('2004-1-2')
      - TO_DAYS('1961-11-15');
```

15388

These functions are designed for use only with Gregorian dates, which begin on 15-Oct-1582. TO_DAYS and FROM_DAYS functions will not return correct results for earlier dates.

Using Unix timestamp support (MySQL)

Use the following functions to convert to and from the Unix timestamp format:

UNIX_TIMESTAMP([*date*])

> Returns a Unix timestamp, which is an unsigned integer with the number of seconds since 1-Jan-1970. With no argument, you get the current timestamp. The *date* argument may be a date string, a datetime string, a timestamp, or their numeric equivalents.

FROM_UNIXTIME(*unix_timestamp*[, *format*]

> Converts a Unix timestamp into a displayable date and time, optionally using the *format* you specify. See the upcoming Table 6 for a list of valid format elements.

For example, to convert 4-Jan-2004 at 7:18 P.M. into the number of seconds since 1-Jan-1970, specify:

```
SELECT UNIX_TIMESTAMP(20040104191800);
```

```
1073261880
```

To convert that timestamp into a human-readable format, specify:

```
SELECT FROM_UNIXTIME(1073261880, '%M %D, %Y at %h:%i:%r');
```

```
January 4th, 2004 at 07:18:07:18:00 PM
```

The *format* argument is optional. The default format for the datetime given in this example is 2004-01-04 19:18:00.

Using seconds-of-the-day (MySQL)

Similar to the Unix timestamp functions that work in terms of seconds since 1-Jan-1970, two MySQL functions let you work in terms of seconds in the day:

SEC_TO_TIME(*seconds*)

> Converts seconds past midnight into a string in the form hh:mi:ss.

```
TIME_TO_SEC(time)
```
Converts a time into seconds past midnight.

For example:

```
SELECT TIME_TO_SEC('19:18');
```

69480

```
SELECT SEC_TO_TIME(69480);
```

19:18:00

Using DATE_FORMAT and TIME_FORMAT (MySQL)

Through the use of *format specifiers*, MySQL provides a great deal of flexibility in converting datetime values into character strings:

```
SELECT DATE_FORMAT(CURRENT_DATE,
       '%W, %M %D, %Y');
```

Sunday, January 4th, 2004

The second argument to DATE_FORMAT is a format string. Format specifiers in that format string are replaced with their respective datetime elements, as described in Table 6. Other text in the format string, such as the commas and spaces in this example, is left in place as part of the function's return value.

TIME_FORMAT works just like DATE_FORMAT, but for time values.

Table 6. MySQL date format specifiers

Specifier	Description
%a	Weekday abbreviation: Sun, Mon, Tue, ...
%b	Month abbreviation: Jan, Feb, Mar, ...
%c	Month number: 1, 2, 3, ...
%D	Day of month with suffix: 1st, 2nd, 3rd, ...
%d	Day of month, two digits: 01, 02, 03, ...

Table 6. MySQL date format specifiers (continued)

Specifier	Description
%e	Day of month: 1, 2, 3, ...
%f	Microseconds: 000000–999999
%H	Hour, two digits, 24-hour clock: 00...23
%h	Hour, two digits, 12-hour clock: 01...12
%j	Day of year: 001...366
%k	Hour, 24-hour clock: 0, 1, ... 23
%l	Hour, 12-hour clock: 1, 2, ... 12
%M	Month name: January, February, ...
%m	Month number: 01, 02, ... 12
%p	Meridian indicator: AM or PM
%r	Time-of-day on a 12-hour clock, e.g., 12:15:05 PM
%S	Seconds: 00, 01, ... 59
%s	Same as %S
%T	Time of day on a 24-hour clock, e.g., 12:15:05 (for 12:15:05 PM)
%U	Week with Sunday as the first day: 00, 01, ... 53
%u	Week with Monday as the first day: 00, 01, ... 53
%V	Week with Sunday as the first day, beginning with 01 and corresponding to %X: 01, 02, ... 53
%v	Week with Monday as the first day, beginning with 01 and corresponding to %x: 01, 02, ... 53
%W	Weekday name: Sunday, Monday, ...
%w	Numeric day of week: 0=Sunday, 1=Monday, ...
%X	Year for the week, four digits, with Sunday as the first day and corresponding to %V
%x	Year for the week, four digits, with Monday as the first day and corresponding to %v
%Y	Four-digit year: 2003, 2004, ...
%y	Two-digit year: 03, 04, ...
%%	Places the percent sign (%) in the output

Numeric Conversions (MySQL)

MySQL implements the following numeric conversion functions:

CONV(*number*, *from_base*, *to_base*)
> Converts a number from one base to another. The *number* may be either an integer or a string, and the base may range from 2 through 36.

BIN(*number*)
> Returns the binary representation of a base-10 *number*.

OCT(*number*)
> Returns the octal representation of a base-10 *number*.

HEX(*number*)
> Returns the hexadecimal representation of a base-10 *number*.

For example:

```
SELECT CONV('AF',16,10);
```

175

```
SELECT HEX(175);
```

AF

Use FORMAT for general-purpose number-to-string conversions. The second argument specifies the number of decimal places in the result:

```
SELECT FORMAT(123456.789,2);
```

123,456.79

Use CAST to convert a string to a number.

Deleting Data

Use the DELETE statement to delete rows from a table. The general syntax is:

```
DELETE
FROM data_source
WHERE predicates
```

DB2 and SQL Server also allow:

```
DELETE
FROM data_source
WHERE CURRENT OF cursor
```

The *data_source* for a DELETE is often a table, but other target types are possible. Ultimately, however, data does get deleted from a table.

TIP

If you're following along by executing the statements I use in examples, I recommend following each example, or set of related examples, with a ROLLBACK.* This will keep your data intact for executing future example code.

Following is an example of a simple DELETE against all rows of a table:

```
DELETE FROM song;
```

More often, you'll write WHERE-clause conditions to identify one or more specific rows to delete. The following query deletes all songs performed by Rondi Olson, and illustrates the use of table aliases. However, note that MySQL and SQL Server 2000 do not support tables aliases in DELETE statements.

```
DELETE FROM song s
WHERE s.artist = 'Rondi Olson';
```

---

* In MySQL, issue the command SET AUTOCOMMIT=0; to enable transactions, and be aware that transactions are not available with the default, MYISAM table type.

If you're processing data through a DB2 cursor, you can delete the row on which the cursor is positioned:

```
DELETE FROM song
WHERE CURRENT OF song_cursor;
```

The following more complex DELETE statement uses a subquery to delete all CDs for which there are no songs:

```
DELETE FROM cd c
WHERE c.cd_id NOT IN (
    SELECT DISTINCT s.cd_id
    FROM song s);
```

Writing a WHERE clause presents the same problem as writing a SELECT statement. See "Predicates" for more details on the different kinds of predicates you can write.

Deleting All Rows

Using a DELETE to remove all rows from a table can be time-consuming and input/output-intensive, as databases must generally log each row deletion. Many databases also implement a TRUNCATE TABLE statement that empties a table more quickly, and without logging.

WARNING

You cannot ROLLBACK a TRUNCATE statement (although in MySQL you can roll back the truncation of an InnoDB table). Table truncation is virtually instantaneous, and it's final.

Following is an example that eliminates all rows from the song table:

```
TRUNCATE TABLE song;
```

Oracle provides a form that preserves any space allocated to the table:

```
TRUNCATE TABLE song REUSE STORAGE;
```

This is a useful form if you plan to immediately reload the table with the same amount of data, because table storage does not need to be deallocated and then reallocated.

As of Version 8.1, DB2 does not support TRUNCATE.

Deleting from Views and Subqueries

The target of a DELETE doesn't have to be a table. It can also be a view or a subquery. For example, the following DELETE eliminates any songs by Carl Behrend that run over five minutes in length:

```
DELETE FROM (
    SELECT *
    FROM song
    WHERE artist = 'Carl Behrend') carls_songs
WHERE carls_songs.playing_time > 300;
```

Databases place various restrictions on deletions from views and subqueries, because ultimately a database must be able to resolve a delete against a view or a subquery to a set of rows in an underlying table. If you can't unambiguously resolve one row in a view or subquery to a corresponding row in one and only one underlying table, then chances are you won't be able to delete from that view or subquery.

NOTE

All of the databases support deleting from a view, but only Oracle supports deleting from a subquery.

Deleting from Partitions (Oracle)

Oracle lets you delete from specific partitions:

```
DELETE
FROM county PARTITION (michigan)
WHERE county_name = 'Alger';
```

or from specific subpartitions:

```
DELETE
FROM county SUBPARTITION (michigan01)
WHERE county_name = 'Alger';
```

But you may be better off not embedding partition and sub-partition names in your SQL statements:

```
DELETE
FROM county
WHERE county_name = 'Alger'
   AND state = 'MI';
```

Each of the three DELETEs in this section will have the same effect. In the third case, Oracle can determine which partition to scan from the WHERE-clause predicate involving state.

Returning the Deleted Data (Oracle)

Oracle supports the following form of DELETE, which returns information about the rows deleted:

```
DELETE FROM ...
WHERE ...
RETURNING expression [,expression...]
[BULK COLLECT] INTO variable [,variable...]
```

The *expression*s would typically be column names, or be built from column names. ROWID is also a valid expression. The target *variable*s must be type-compatible PL/SQL or bind variables.

For DELETEs of more than one row, the target variables must also be PL/SQL collection types, and you must use the BULK COLLECT keywords:

```
DECLARE
   TYPE county_id_array IS ARRAY(100) OF NUMBER;
   county_ids county_id_array;
BEGIN
   DELETE FROM county
   RETURNING county_id BULK COLLECT INTO county_ids;
END;
/
```

Rather than specifying a target *variable* for each source *expression*, your target can be a record containing the appropriate number and type of fields.

Double-FROM (SQL Server)

SQL Server supports an odd extension to DELETE that lets you delete from the results of a table join. For example, to delete all songs on CDs with a price higher than $10.00, specify:

```
DELETE FROM song
FROM cd c INNER JOIN song s
     ON c.cd_id = s.cd_id
WHERE c.price > 10;
```

In this syntax, the first FROM clause identifies the ultimate target of the DELETE. The second FROM clause specifies a table join. Predicates in the WHERE clause can then evaluate columns from both tables in the join. In this example, rows are deleted from the song table based on a price in the cd table.

The first FROM keyword is optional, and is often omitted:

```
DELETE song
FROM cd c INNER JOIN song s
...
```

If you're not using SQL Server or you wish to avoid proprietary extensions to SQL, you can accomplish the same kind of DELETE via a subquery, using ANSI-standard SQL:

```
DELETE FROM song
WHERE song.cd_id IN (
    SELECT cd.cd_id
    FROM cd
    WHERE cd.price > 10);
```

or:

```
DELETE FROM song
WHERE EXISTS (
    SELECT * FROM cd
    WHERE cd.price > 10
      AND cd.cd_id = song.cd_id);
```

Flashback Queries (Oracle)

Oracle9i Database, Release 2 introduced the concept of a *flashback query*, which lets you query data as it existed at some point in the past.

Use the AS OF keyword following a table name in the FROM clause to initiate a flashback query:

```
SELECT a.attraction_name
FROM attraction
AS OF TIMESTAMP TIMESTAMP '2003-05-20 15:00:00.00' a
WHERE a.city_id=1;
```

Note the location of the table alias. Be sure to place the AS OF between the table name and any alias you want to give that table in your query.

The double occurrence of the TIMESTAMP keyword is no error. AS OF TIMESTAMP specifies that you will supply the flashback target in the form of a timestamp, which you can supply either in a variable or as a literal. The examples in this section use TIMESTAMP literals, which begin with that keyword.

You can specify different AS OF parameters, or none at all, for each table (or view) in your query:

```
SELECT a.attraction_name, c.city_name
FROM attraction
   AS OF TIMESTAMP
      TIMESTAMP '2003-05-20 15:00:00.00' a
   INNER JOIN city
   AS OF TIMESTAMP
      TIMESTAMP '2003-05-20 03:00:00.00' c
   ON a.city_id = c.city_id;
```

Rather than go by timestamp, you can base a flashback query on a system change number (SCN):

```
SELECT attraction_name, city_name
FROM city c, (SELECT *
              FROM attraction
              WHERE government_owned = 'Y')
              AS OF SCN 69335732 a
WHERE c.city_id = a.city_id(+);
```

System change numbers are much more precise than time-stamps for specifying flashback targets. Timestamps are ultimately resolved to SCNs recorded at five-minute intervals, and that history goes back for only five days of database operation.

Functions

Database vendors implement large numbers of functions that you can use from within SQL statements to manipulate and transform data. For example, you can use the UPPER function from within a SQL statement to search in a case-insensitive manner:

```
SELECT artist, title
FROM cd
WHERE UPPER(title) = 'NOTHING LESS';
```

Be aware that applying a function to a column in a WHERE or HAVING clause *may* prevent the use of an index on that column. For example, if the cd table is indexed by title, the use of a function in this example will block the use of that index. On the other hand, if the table is indexed by UPPER(title) via a functional index, then the preceding query can take advantage of that index. Because of this issue, you may be better off finding ways to write your queries without applying functions to critical search columns in your WHERE clause.

There are many different types of functions. The following sections describe the more useful *scalar functions*, which return one value per row when issued from a SQL statement. These fall into several categories:

- Date functions
- Numeric and math functions
- Trigonometric functions
- String functions

There are also a few functions that don't fit into any of these categories. By far the most useful are *conversion functions* that convert data from one type to another. See the earlier section "Datatype Conversion" to learn more about those functions. There are also *aggregate functions*, which combine values from many rows to return one result. These are described in the later section "Grouping and Summarizing."

Date Functions

As mentioned previously, the most useful date functions are actually conversion functions, described earlier under "Datatype Conversion." Even so, there are a few other datetime functions you should know about.

Getting the current date and time

Every database vendor implements one or more functions to return the current date, the current time, both date and time, or variations on that theme. Oracle, for example, implements SYSDATE to return a DATE value with the current server operating-system date and time:

```
SQL> ALTER SESSION
  2  SET NLS_DATE_FORMAT = 'dd-Mon-yyyy hh:mi:ss';

Session altered.

SQL> SELECT SYSDATE FROM dual;

SYSDATE
-------------------
31-Dec-2003 06:24:15
```

Oracle current date/time functions. Oracle implements the following functions to return current datetime information:

CURRENT_DATE
Returns the current date in the session time zone as a value of type DATE.

CURRENT_TIMESTAMP[(*precision*)]
Returns the current date and time in the session time zone as a value of type TIMESTAMP WITH TIME

ZONE. The precision is the number of decimal digits used to express fractional seconds, and defaults to 6.

LOCALTIMESTAMP[(*precision*)]
Same as CURRENT_TIMESTAMP, but returns a TIMESTAMP value with no time zone offset.

SYSDATE
Returns the server date and time as a DATE.

SYSTIMESTAMP[(*precision*)]
Returns the current server date and time as a TIMESTAMP WITH TIME ZONE value.

DBTIMEZONE
Returns the database server time zone as an offset from UTC in the form [+|-]hh:mi.

SESSIONTIMEZONE
Returns the session time zone as an offset from UTC in the form [+|-]hh:mi.

SYS_EXTRACT_UTC(*datetime*)
Returns the UTC date and time from a TIMESTAMP WITH TIME ZONE value.

DB2 current date/time functions. DB2 implements what IBM refers to as *special registers* to return datetime information:

CURRENT DATE *or* CURRENT_DATE
Returns the current date on the server.

CURRENT TIME *or* CURRENT_TIME
Returns the current time on the server.

CURRENT TIMESTAMP *or* CURRENT_TIMESTAMP
Returns the current date and time as a timestamp.

CURRENT TIMEZONE *or* CURRENT_TIMEZONE
Returns the current time zone as a decimal number representing the time zone offset, in hours, minutes, and seconds, from UTC. The first two digits are the hours; the second two digits are the minutes; the last two digits are the seconds.

SQL Server current date/time functions. SQL Server implements:

CURRENT_TIMESTAMP *or* GETDATE( )
> Returns the current date and time on the server as a datetime value.

GETUTCDATE( )
> Returns the current UTC date and time, as derived from the server's time and time zone setting.

MySQL current date/time functions. MySQL implements:

CURDATE( ) *or* CURRENT_DATE
> Returns the current date as a string ('YYYY-MM-DD') or a number (YYYYMMDD), depending on the context.

CURTIME( ) *or* CURRENT_TIME
> Returns the current time as a string ('HH:MI:SS') or a number (HHMISS), depending on the context.

NOW( ), SYSDATE( ), *or* CURRENT_TIMESTAMP
> Returns the current date and time as a string ('YYYY-MM-DD HH:MI:SS') or a number (YYYYMMDDHHMISS), depending on the context.

UNIX_TIMESTAMP
> Returns the number of seconds since the beginning of 1-Jan-1970 as an integer.

Rounding and truncating (Oracle)

Oracle allows you to round and truncate DATE values to specific datetime elements. The following example illustrates rounding and truncating to the nearest month:

```
SQL> SELECT SYSDATE, ROUND(SYSDATE,'Mon'),
  2         TRUNC(SYSDATE,'Mon')
  3  FROM dual;

SYSDATE     ROUND(SYSDA TRUNC(SYSDA
----------- ----------- -----------
31-Dec-2003 01-Jan-2004 01-Dec-2003
```

Truncation simply sets any element of lesser significance than the one you specify to its minimum value. The minimum day value is 1, so 31-Dec was truncated to 1-Dec. Had my output format included the time of day, you would see that it had been truncated to 00:00:00, or midnight beginning the day.

Rounding is done to the nearest occurrence of the element you specify. I asked to round to the nearest month. My input date was closer to 1-Jan-2004 than it was to 1-Dec-2003, so my date was rounded up. Again, the time of day would be set to 00:00:00.

You can use the date format elements from Table 1, under "Datatype Conversion," to specify the element to which you want to round or truncate a date. Avoid the esoteric elements such as RM (Roman numerals) and J (Julian day); stick to easily understood elements such as MM (month), Q (quarter), and so forth. If you omit the second argument to ROUND or TRUNC, the rounding or truncating is done to the day (the DD element).

Useful date functions (Oracle)

Oracle implements several useful functions for performing date arithmetic. The following functions all work with, and usually return, values of type DATE:

ADD_MONTHS(*date, integer*)
   Adds *integer* months to *date*. If *date* is the last day of its month, the result is forced to the last day of the target month. If the target month has fewer days than *date*'s month, the result is also forced to the last of the month.

LAST_DAY(*date*)
   Returns the last day of the month that contains a *date* that you specify.

NEXT_DAY(*date, weekday*)
   Returns the first specified weekday following a given *date*. The *weekday* must be a valid weekday name or

abbreviation in the current date language for the session. (You can query NLS_SESSION_PARAMETERS to check this value.) Even when *date* falls on *weekday*, the function will still return the *next* occurrence of *weekday*.

MONTHS_BETWEEN(*later_date*, *earlier_date*)

Computes the number of months between two dates. The math corresponds to *later_date – earlier_date*. The input dates can actually be in any order, but if the second date is later, the result will be negative.

The result will be an integer number of months for any case in which both dates correspond to the same day of the month, or for any case in which both dates correspond to the last day of their respective months. Otherwise, Oracle calculates a fractional result based on a 31-day month, also considering any time-of-day components of the input dates.

Useful date functions (SQL Server)

SQL Server implements two functions for performing date arithmetic:

DATEADD(*datepart*, *interval*, *date*)

Adds an interval (expressed as an integer) to a *date*. Specify a negative interval to perform subtraction. The *datepart* argument is a keyword specifying the portion of the *date* to increment, and may be any of year, yy, yyyy, quarter, qq, q, month, mm, m, dayofyear, dy, y, day, dd, d, week, wk, ww, hour, hh, minute, mi, n, second, ss, s, millisecond, and ms. For example, to add one day to the current date, use DATEADD(day, 1, GETDATE( )).

DATEDIFF(*datepart*, *startdate*, *enddate*)

Returns *enddate – startdate* expressed in terms of the units you specify for the *datepart* argument. For example, to compute the number of minutes between the current time and UTC time, use DATEDIFF(mi, GETUTCDATE( ), GETDATE( )).

Useful date functions (MySQL)

MySQL implements the following functions for adding and subtracting intervals from dates.

DATE_ADD(*date*, INTERVAL *value units*)
    Adds *value* number of *units* to the *date*. You can use ADDDATE as a synonym for DATE_ADD.

DATE_SUB(*date*, INTERVAL *value units*)
    Subtracts *value* number of *units* from the *date*. You can use SUBDATE as a synonym for DATE_SUB.

For example, to add one month to the current date:

```
SELECT DATE_ADD(CURRENT_DATE, INTERVAL 1 MONTH);
```

Or, to subtract one year and two months:

```
SELECT DATE_SUB(CURRENT_DATE,
                INTERVAL '1-2' YEAR_MONTH);
```

Valid interval keywords for numeric intervals include SEC-OND, MINUTE, HOUR, DAY, MONTH, and YEAR. You can also use the string-based formats shown in Table 7.

Table 7. MySQL string-based interval formats

Keyword	Format
DAY_HOUR	'dd hh'
DAY_MINUTE	'dd hh:mi'
DAY_SECOND	'dd hh:mi:ss'
HOUR_MINUTE	'HH:MI'
HOUR_SECOND	'hh:mi:ss'
MINUTE_SECOND	'MI:SS'
YEAR_MONTH	'yy-mm'

Numeric and Math Functions

Following are some useful numeric and math functions that are fairly universal across database platforms (I note any platform limitations):

ABS(*number*)
> Returns the absolute value of *number*.

CEIL(*number*) *or* CEILING(*number*)
> Returns the smallest integer that is greater than or equal to the number that you pass. Use CEILING for SQL Server, CEIL for other platforms. Remember that with negative numbers, the *greater* value has the lower *absolute* value. CEIL(5.5) is 6, whereas CEIL(-5.5) is -5.

EXP(*number*)
> Returns the mathematical constant e (≈ 2.71828183) raised to the *number*th power.

FLOOR(*number*)
> Returns the largest integer that is less than or equal to the number you pass. Remember that with negative numbers, the *lesser* value has the higher *absolute* value. FLOOR(5.5) is 5, whereas FLOOR(-5.5) is -6.

LN(*number*)
> Returns the natural logarithm of a number. Available in Oracle and DB2, but not in SQL Server and MySQL.

LOG(*number*)
> A DB2, SQL Server, and MySQL function that returns the natural logarithm of a *number*.

LOG(*base, number*)
> An Oracle function that returns the logarithm of a *number* in a *base* that you specify.

LOG10(*number*)
> A DB2, SQL Server, and MySQL function that returns the base-10 logarithm of a *number*.

MOD(*top, bottom*)

Returns the remainder of *top* divided by *bottom*. Available in Oracle, DB2, and MySQL, but not in SQL Server.

NANVL(*value, alternate*)

An Oracle function that returns an alternate value for any floating-point NaN (Not-a-Number) *value*. If *value* is NaN, then *alternate* is returned; otherwise, *value* is returned.

REMAINDER(*top, bottom*)

An Oracle function that returns the remainder of *top* divided by *bottom*, the same as MOD.

ROUND(*number*[, *places*])

Rounds a *number* to a specified number of decimal *places*. The default is to round to an integer value. Use a negative value for *places* to round to the *left* of the decimal point. SQL Server requires the *places* argument.

ROUND(*number, places*[, *option*])

SQL Server's version of ROUND. Use *option* to specify whether rounding or truncating is performed (see TRUNC below). If *option* is 0, the function rounds; otherwise, the function truncates.

SIGN(*number*)

Indicates the sign of a number. SIGN returns −1, 0, or 1 depending on whether *number* is negative, zero, or positive.

TRUNC(*number*[, *precision*])

Truncates a number to a specific number of decimal places. The default *precision* is zero decimal places. Use a negative *precision* to truncate to the left of the decimal point, forcing those digits to zero. SQL Server implements truncation using a special form of ROUND. MySQL implements truncation using TRUNCATE(*number, precision*), requiring that you specify *precision*.

Trigonometric Functions

All of the database platforms offer a suite of trigonometric functions; the exact functions vary from one database to the next, and are listed in Table 8. If you're familiar with trigonometry, the purpose of each function will be readily apparent from its name.

Table 8. Trigonometric functions

Function	Oracle	DB2	SQL Server	MySQL
ACOS(*cosine*)	•	•	•	•
ASIN(*sine*)	•	•	•	•
ATAN(*tangent*)	•	•	•	•
ATANH(*htangent*)		•		
COS(*radians*)	•	•	•	•
COSH(*radians*)	•	•		
COT(*radians*)		•	•	•
SIN(*radians*)	•	•	•	•
SINH(*radians*)	•	•		
TAN(*radians*)	•	•	•	•
TANH(*radians*)	•	•		

There is also a special form of ATAN known as ATAN2 (ATN2 in SQL Server):

    ATAN2(x, y)

The function returns ATAN(x/y).

String Functions

The following sections show how to use functions to perform common string operations.

Searching a string

Different databases provide different functions for searching a string.

Oracle search function. In Oracle, use the INSTR function to find the location of a substring within a string:

```
INSTR(string, substring[, position[, occurrence]])
```

You can optionally specify a starting *position* for the search, and you can request that a specific *occurrence* be found. In Oracle, if *position* is negative, the search begins from the end of the string.

TIP

In Oracle Database 10g, you can also use REGEXP_INSTR, as described under "Regular Expressions."

Oracle implements INSTR, INSTRB, INSTR2, and INSTR4, which work in terms of the input character set, bytes, Unicode code units, and Unicode code points, respectively.

DB2 search function. In DB2, use the LOCATE function:

```
LOCATE(substring, string[, position]]))
```

LOCATE returns the first occurrence of *substring* within *string*. Zero is returned if no match is found. The default is to search *string* beginning from character position 1.

SQL Server search function. In SQL Server, use the CHARINDEX function:

```
CHARINDEX(substring, string[, position]]))
```

The arguments are the same as for DB2's LOCATE.

MySQL search functions. In MySQL, use either INSTR or LOCATE:

```
INSTR(string, substring)
LOCATE(substring, string[, position])
```

Use *position* to specify a starting character position other than 1. Zero is returned if *substring* is not found within *string*.

Replacing text in a string

Use the REPLACE function to perform a search-and-replace operation on a *string*:

```
REPLACE(string, search[, replace])
```

If you omit the *replace*ment string, you'll delete all occurrences of *search* within *string*. In DB2, SQL Server, and MySQL you *must* supply all three arguments, but you can still delete a substring by specifying an empty string ('') as the *replace* text.

TIP

In Oracle Database 10g, you can also use REGEXP_REPLACE, as described under "Regular Expressions."

Extracting a substring

In Oracle, DB2, and SQL Server, use the SUBSTR function to extract *length* characters from a *string*, beginning at position *start*:

```
SUBSTR(string, start[, length])
```

Strings begin with position 1. Oracle treats a *start* of 0 as if you had specified 1. If *start* is negative, Oracle counts backward from the end of the *string*.

Omit *length* to get all characters from *start* to the end of the *string*. DB2 pads any result with spaces, if necessary, to ensure the result is always *length* characters long. SQL Server does not allow you to omit *length*.

TIP

In Oracle Database 10g, you can also use REGEXP_SUBSTR, as described under "Regular Expressions."

Oracle implements SUBSTR, SUBSTRB, SUBSTR2, and SUBSTR4, which work in terms of the input character set, bytes, Unicode code units, and Unicode code points, respectively.

MySQL implements the following substring functions:

```
SUBSTRING(string, start)
SUBSTRING(string FROM start)
SUBSTRING(string, start, length)
SUBSTRING(string FROM start FOR length)
```

The arguments to these SUBSTRING functions are the same as for SUBSTR. MySQL supports a negative start position, which counts from the right.

Finding the length of a string

Use the LENGTH function (LEN in SQL Server) to determine the length of a string:

```
LENGTH(string)
```

Oracle implements LENGTH, LENGTHB, LENGTH2, and LENGTH4, which count characters in the input character set, bytes, Unicode code units, and Unicode code points, respectively.

Concatenating strings

In Oracle and DB2, you can use the CONCAT function to concatenate two strings:

```
CONCAT(string, string)
```

However, you'll likely find it easier to use the string concatenation operator (||) instead:

```
string1 || string2
```

SQL Server does not support the ANSI/ISO string concatenation operator. Use a + instead.

MySQL supports neither || nor + for concatenating strings. However, MySQL supports an unlimited number of string arguments to CONCAT:

```
CONCAT(string[, string...])
```

Trimming unwanted characters

LTRIM, RTRIM, and TRIM remove unwanted characters from a string. TRIM is part of the ANSI/ISO standard, though it is not supported by DB2 Version 8.1 or SQL Server 2000:

```
TRIM(string)
TRIM(character FROM string)
TRIM(option [character] FROM string)

option ::= {LEADING|TRAILING|BOTH}
```

Using TRIM, you can trim leading characters, trailing characters, or both from a string. The character to trim defaults to a single space. The default option is BOTH.

The LTRIM and RTRIM functions provide similar functionality to TRIM. Oracle's implementation is:

```
LTRIM(string[, unwanted])
RTRIM(string[, unwanted])
```

The implementations for DB2, SQL Server, and MySQL are:

```
LTRIM(string)
RTRIM(string)
```

LTRIM removes unwanted characters from the beginning (left edge) of a string, while RTRIM removes from the end (right edge). The unwanted argument is a string containing the characters you want trimmed, and defaults to a single space. In DB2, SQL Server, and MySQL you can trim only spaces.

TRIM lets you specify only one character to remove. With Oracle's versions of LTRIM and RTRIM, you can remove many characters at once simply by listing them all in the unwanted string. For example, to remove some leading and trailing punctuation and spaces:

```
RTRIM(LTRIM(string,'.,! '),'.,! ')
```

Translating characters

Oracle and DB2 implement a TRANSLATE function to translate characters in a string. Oracle's implementation is:

```
TRANSLATE(string, original, translation)
```

DB2 implements a somewhat more complex version:

```
TRANSLATE(string)
TRANSLATE(string, translation, original[, pad]))
```

The function searches *string*, replacing each occurrence of a character found in *original* with the corresponding character from *translation*. For example, to change all digits to the letters A through J, specify:

```
SQL> SELECT TRANSLATE('This book costs $9.95.',
  2                   '1234567890','ABCDEFGHIJ')
  3  FROM dual;

TRANSLATE('THISBOOKCOS
----------------------
This book costs $I.IE.
```

In Oracle, characters in *string* but not in *original* are left untouched. Characters in *original* but not in *translation* are deleted.

In DB2, the *pad* character is used to pad *translation* to at least the length of *original*. Any characters in *original* but not in *translation* are translated to the *pad* character. The default *pad* character is a space. If *translation* is longer than *original*, those extra characters are ignored.

Changing the case of a string

Use the UPPER and LOWER functions to uppercase or lowercase all letters in a string:

```
UPPER(string)
LOWER(string)
```

In Oracle, you can also use INITCAP(*string*) to uppercase the first letter of each word in a string and lowercase the other letters.

DB2 supports UCASE and LCASE as synonyms for UPPER and LOWER.

Miscellaneous Functions (Oracle)

Oracle implements two functions that don't fall into the date, numeric, or string categories, but are still of interest:

GREATEST(*value*[, *value*...])
> Returns the greatest value from a list of values. The input values may be numbers, dates, or strings.

LEAST(*value*[, *value*...])
> Returns the least value from a list of values. The input values may be numbers, dates, or strings.

Grouping and Summarizing

SQL enables you to group rows into sets and then to summarize that data in various ways, ultimately returning just one row per set. You do this using the GROUP BY and HAVING clauses, and various aggregate functions.

Aggregate Functions

An *aggregate function* takes as input a set of values, one from each row in a group of rows, and returns one value as output. One of the most common aggregate functions is COUNT, which counts non-NULL values in a column. The following statement counts the number of attraction URLs:

```
SELECT COUNT(attraction_url)
FROM attraction;
```

Use the ALL and DISTINCT keywords to control whether all non-NULL values are used as input, or whether duplicate values are excluded:

```
SELECT COUNT(DISTINCT city_id),
       COUNT(ALL city_id)
FROM attraction;
```

The ALL behavior is the default: COUNT(*expression*) is equivalent to COUNT(ALL *expression*).

COUNT is a special case in that it lets you pass the asterisk (*) as a wildcard argument:

```
SELECT COUNT(*) FROM attraction;
```

When you use COUNT(*), SQL counts rows rather than column values. NULLity is irrelevant when COUNT(*) is used because the concept of NULL applies only to columns, not to entire rows as a whole.

Table 9 lists some commonly available aggregate functions; most database vendors implement aggregate functions beyond those shown. Oracle is notable for supporting not only a long list of aggregate functions, but also some rather complex calling syntax; check their documentation for details.

Table 9. Common aggregate functions

Function	Description
AVG(x)	Returns the average (mean) of a set of numbers.
COUNT(x)	Counts the number of non-NULL values in a set of values.
MAX(x)	Returns the greatest value in a set.
MEDIAN(x)	Returns the median, or middle value, from a set of values. The middle value may be interpolated. Available only for Oracle.
MIN(x)	Returns the least value in a set.
STDDEV(x)	Returns the standard deviation of a set of numbers. Use STDEV (only one D) in SQL Server.
SUM(x)	Sums all numbers in a set.
VARIANCE(x)	Returns the statistical variance of the numbers in a set. Use VAR in SQL Server. Not available in DB2 or MySQL.

GROUP BY

Aggregate functions really come into their own when you apply them to groups of rows rather than to all rows in a table. Do this using the GROUP BY clause. The following query counts the number of attractions in each city:

```
SELECT c.city_name, COUNT(*)
FROM city c INNER JOIN attraction a
    ON c.city_id = a.city_id
GROUP BY c.city_name;
```

When executing a query like this, the database first sorts result-set rows into groups as specified by the GROUP BY clause:

Munising	Pictured Rocks
Munising	Valley Spur
Munising	Shipwreck Tours
Gladstone	Hoegh Pet Casket Company
Hancock	Quincy Steam Hoist
Hancock	Temple Jacob
Hancock	Finlandia University
Germfask	Seney National Wildlife Refuge

...

Groups may consist of only one row. Grouping usually implies at least a limited sort operation, but as you can see from this example, sorting needs to proceed only to the point where like rows are grouped together.

After the groups have been created, any aggregate functions are applied once to each group. In this example, COUNT(*) is evaluated separately for each group:

Munising	3
Munising	
Munising	
Gladstone	1
Hancock	3
Hancock	
Hancock	
Germfask	1

...

Any columns to which an aggregate function has not been applied are now "collapsed" into one value:

```
Munising      3
Gladstone     1
Hancock       3
Germfask      1
...
```

In practical terms, this collapsing of many detail rows into one aggregate row means that you *must* apply an aggregate function to any column not listed in your GROUP BY clause.

Useful GROUP BY Techniques

The following subsections describe some useful techniques for writing GROUP BY queries.

Reducing the GROUP BY list

Sometimes you want to list a column in the SELECT list of a GROUP BY query without having to list that same column in the GROUP BY clause. For example, in the following query a given city_id implies a city_name:

```
SELECT c.city_id, c.city_name, COUNT(*)
FROM city c INNER JOIN attraction a
     ON c.city_id = a.city_id
GROUP BY c.city_id, c.city_name;
```

In a case like this, rather than grouping by two columns, it might be more efficient to group by only the city_id column, yielding a much shorter sort key. The grouping sort will potentially run faster and use less scratch space on disk. One approach to doing this is as follows:

```
SELECT c.city_id, MAX(c.city_name), COUNT(*)
FROM city c INNER JOIN attraction a
     ON c.city_id = a.city_id
GROUP BY c.city_id;
```

I've dropped the city_name column from the GROUP BY clause. To compensate for that, I've arbitrarily applied the MAX function to that same column in the SELECT list. This satisfies the rule that all non–GROUP BY expressions must be enclosed in an aggregate function, while at the same time giving a usable city name. Because all city names within a group of like city_id values are the same, MAX can only return that one name.

Grouping before the join

The GROUP BY examples in the preceding section involve a join that is performed prior to the grouping operation. Using a subquery, it's possible to restate the query in a way that causes the join to occur after the aggregation rather than before:

```
SELECT c.city_name, agg.attcount
FROM city c INNER JOIN (
    SELECT city_id, COUNT(*) attcount
    FROM attraction
    GROUP BY city_id) agg
ON c.city_id = agg.city_id;
```

The advantage here is that the join involves far fewer rows because the aggregation occurs prior to the join, not after. A further advantage is a potential reduction in scratch disk and memory requirements, as the rows involved in the GROUP BY operation and subsequent aggregation do not include any data from the city table.

HAVING

Use the HAVING clause to place restrictions on the rows returned from a GROUP BY query. For example, to list only those cities having more than one attraction, specify:

```
SELECT c.city_name, COUNT(*)
FROM city c INNER JOIN attraction a
    ON c.city_id = a.city_id
GROUP BY c.city_name
HAVING COUNT(*) > 1;
```

Never put a condition in the HAVING clause that does not involve an aggregation. Consider the following query to list the number of attractions in the cities of the Keweenaw Peninsula:

```
SELECT c.city_name, COUNT(*)
FROM city c INNER JOIN attraction a
    ON c.city_id = a.city_id
GROUP BY c.city_name
HAVING c.city_name IN
    ('Copper Harbor', 'Hancock');
```

This query is much more efficiently expressed with the restriction on city name in the WHERE clause:

```
SELECT c.city_name, COUNT(*)
FROM city c INNER JOIN attraction a
    ON c.city_id = a.city_id
WHERE c.city_name IN
    ('Copper Harbor', 'Hancock')
GROUP BY c.city_name;
```

The WHERE clause reduces the number of rows going into the GROUP BY operation. Fewer rows need to be sorted, and fewer aggregations need to be performed. Use the HAVING clause to filter rows coming out of the GROUP BY operation when you need to filter on aggregated values.

GROUP BY Extensions (Oracle)

Oracle implements several useful GROUP BY extensions: ROLLUP, CUBE, and GROUPING SETS. The following sections describe these functions, as well as some scalar functions that help you manage the results of Oracle's extensions.

ROLLUP (Oracle)

The ROLLUP operation generates a summary row for each group:

```
SELECT cy.county_name, c.city_name,
    COUNT(a.attraction_id) cnt
FROM (county cy INNER JOIN city c
    ON cy.county_id = c.county_id)
    INNER JOIN attraction a
    ON c.city_id = a.city_id
```

```
GROUP BY ROLLUP(cy.county_name, c.city_name)
HAVING COUNT(a.attraction_id) > 1;
```

Following is the output from this query. The rows in bold-face are those generated as a result of using ROLLUP:

COUNTY_NAME	CITY_NAME	CNT
Alger	Munising	3
Alger		**3**
Houghton	Hancock	3
Houghton		**3**
Marquette	Ishpeming	2
Marquette	Marquette	3
Marquette		**5**
		20

The GROUP BY operation generated the normal summary by city. The ROLLUP operation added in summaries for all other possible levels: by county, and for the entire set of rows. Notice that Marquette County has five attractions, and that there are 20 attractions in all.

You don't need to ROLLUP by all the GROUP BY columns. The following clause results in counts for each city and each county, but omits the grand-total row generated by the previous example:

```
GROUP BY cy.county_name, ROLLUP(c.city_name)
```

CUBE (Oracle)

CUBE takes things a step further. It generates summaries for all possible combinations of the columns you specify, and also a grand total:

```
SELECT cy.county_name, c.city_name,
       COUNT(a.attraction_id) cnt
FROM (county cy INNER JOIN city c
    ON cy.county_id = c.county_id)
    INNER JOIN attraction a
    ON c.city_id = a.city_id
WHERE cy.county_name = 'Houghton'
GROUP BY CUBE(cy.county_name, c.city_name);
```

COUNTY_NAME	CITY_NAME	CNT
		3
	Hancock	3
Houghton		3
Houghton	Hancock	3

GROUPING SETS (Oracle)

Introduced in Oracle9i, GROUPING SETS lets you specify the groupings that you want:

```
SELECT cy.county_name, c.city_name,
       COUNT(a.attraction_id) cnt
FROM (county cy INNER JOIN city c
    ON cy.county_id = c.county_id)
    INNER JOIN attraction a
    ON c.city_id = a.city_id
GROUP BY
   GROUPING SETS(cy.county_name, c.city_name)
HAVING COUNT(a.attraction_id) > 1;
```

COUNTY_NAME	CITY_NAME	CNT
Alger		3
Houghton		3
Marquette		5
	Hancock	3
	Ishpeming	2
	Marquette	3
	Munising	3

Here, GROUPING SETS generates aggregations by county and by city. Without GROUPING SETS, you would need to issue two queries to get this same information.

Related functions (Oracle)

The following functions are useful when using Oracle's extended GROUP BY features:

GROUPING(column)

Returns 1 if a NULL column value was the result of a CUBE, ROLLUP, or GROUPING SETS operation; otherwise returns 0.

```
GROUPING_ID(column, column, ...)
```
Similar to GROUPING, but generates a bit vector of 1s and 0s depending on whether the corresponding columns contain NULLs generated by an extended GROUP BY feature. Available in Oracle9*i* and higher.

```
GROUP_ID( )
```
Enables you to distinguish between duplicate rows in the output from CUBE, ROLLUP, and GROUPING SETS. The function returns 0 through *n*–1 for each row in a set of *n* duplicates. You can use that return value to decide how many duplicates to retain. Use HAVING GROUP_ID( )=0 to eliminate all duplicates.

GROUP BY Extensions (SQL Server)

SQL Server also implements the GROUP BY extensions CUBE and ROLLUP, but in a slightly different and somewhat less flexible manner than Oracle does.

ROLLUP (SQL Server)

Use ROLLUP to generate a summary row for each group:

```
SELECT cy.county_name, c.city_name,
       COUNT(a.attraction_id) cnt
FROM (county cy INNER JOIN city c
    ON cy.county_id = c.county_id)
    INNER JOIN attraction a
    ON c.city_id = a.city_id
GROUP BY cy.county_name, c.city_name WITH ROLLUP
HAVING COUNT(a.attraction_id) > 1;
```

The results from this statement are the same as for the Oracle ROLLUP query shown earlier. With SQL Server, however, you cannot ROLLUP only some of the GROUP BY columns. It's all or none.

CUBE (SQL Server)

Use CUBE to generate summaries for all possible combinations of GROUP BY columns, as well as a grand total:

```
SELECT cy.county_name, c.city_name,
       COUNT(a.attraction_id) cnt
FROM (county cy INNER JOIN city c
    ON cy.county_id = c.county_id)
    INNER JOIN attraction a
    ON c.city_id = a.city_id
WHERE cy.county_name = 'Houghton'
GROUP BY cy.county_name, c.city_name WITH CUBE;
```

The results are the same as for the Oracle CUBE query shown earlier. And just as with ROLLUP, you cannot apply CUBE to a subset of GROUP BY columns.

GROUPING (SQL Server)

SQL Server supports the same GROUPING function that Oracle does: it returns 1 or 0 depending on whether a NULL value is the result of a CUBE or ROLLUP operation. For example:

```
SELECT cy.county_name, c.city_name,
       COUNT(a.attraction_id) cnt,
       GROUPING(cy.county_name) n1,
       GROUPING(c.city_name) n2
FROM (county cy INNER JOIN city c
    ON cy.county_id = c.county_id)
    INNER JOIN attraction a
    ON c.city_id = a.city_id
WHERE cy.county_name = 'Houghton'
GROUP BY cy.county_name, c.city_name WITH CUBE;
```

In this query, the two GROUPING calls will return 1 whenever their associated columns in the result set contain a NULL value generated by the CUBE operation.

COUNTY_NAME	CITY_NAME	CNT	N1	N2
Houghton	Hancock	3	0	0
Houghton	NULL	3	0	1
NULL	NULL	3	1	1
NULL	Hancock	3	1	0

Hierarchical Queries

ANSI/ISO and Oracle provide different syntax for querying data in a recursive, parent-child relationship. A stereotypical example of such a relationship is a bill of materials, in which one assembly is composed of subassemblies composed of more subassemblies, on down an indeterminate number of levels until you reach discrete parts at the bottom.

ANSI/ISO Recursive WITH (DB2)

DB2 supports the ANSI/ISO recursive use of WITH for querying hierarchical and recursive data. For example, to query the bill-of-materials structure in the bill_of_materials table, you could write:

```
WITH recursiveBOM
    (level, assembly_id, assembly_name,
     parent_assembly) AS
(SELECT 1,
        parent.assembly_id,
        parent.assembly_name,
        parent.parent_assembly
FROM bill_of_materials parent
WHERE parent.assembly_id=100
UNION ALL
SELECT parent.level+1,
        child.assembly_id,
        child.assembly_name,
        child.parent_assembly
FROM recursiveBOM parent, bill_of_materials child
WHERE child.parent_assembly = parent.assembly_id)
SELECT level, assembly_id,
        parent_assembly, assembly_name
FROM recursiveBOM;
```

Most of this statement consists of a subquery named recursiveBOM that is specified using the WITH clause. The subquery consists of two SELECTs unioned together:

- Consider the first SELECT as the union query's starting point.
- Consider the second SELECT as defining the recursive link between parent and child rows.

The second SELECT brings in the children of the first. Because the second SELECT references the named subquery that it is part of (itself), the second SELECT recursively brings back rows returned by the second SELECT. The main SELECT kicks off all this recursion by simply selecting from the named subquery.

TIP

For a more in-depth explanation of what happens when a recursive WITH executes, read the article "Understanding the WITH Clause" at *http://gennick.com/with*.

DB2 returns recursive results in the following order, which differs from the order you'll get from Oracle:

1. The root node
2. The root's immediate children
3. The children of the root's immediate children
4. And so forth.

To keep track of your depth in a hierarchy, create a LEVEL column as shown in the example query. Have the first SELECT return 1 as the value for that column. Have the second SELECT return parent.level+1. The root node will then have a level of 1, the root's immediate children will be level 2, and so on, down to the bottom of the hierarchy.

CONNECT BY Syntax (Oracle)

Use the CONNECT BY syntax and related functions to write recursive queries in Oracle. While Oracle does not support ANSI's recursive use of WITH, Oracle's CONNECT BY feature set is arguably more expressive and easier to use.

CONNECT BY, START WITH, and PRIOR (Oracle)

To return data in a hierarchy, specify a starting node using START WITH and specify the parent-child relationship using CONNECT BY:

```
SELECT assembly_id, assembly_name, parent_assembly
FROM bill_of_materials
START WITH assembly_id = 100
CONNECT BY parent_assembly = PRIOR assembly_id;
```

```
ASSEMBLY_ID ASSEMBLY_NAME              PARENT_ASSEMBLY
----------- ----------------------    ---------------
        100 Automobile
        110 Combustion Engine                     100
        111 Piston                                110
        112 Air Filter                            110
        113 Spark Plug                            110
        114 Block                                 110
        115 Starter System                        110
        116 Alternator                            115
        117 Battery                               115
        118 Starter Motor                         115
...
```

The START WITH clause specifies the first row Oracle looks at. In this example, the database begins with assembly #100, the automobile. Use the CONNECT BY clause to specify the relationship between parent and child rows. In this bill of materials, as you navigate down the hierarchy, each child's parent_assembly must equal the parent's assembly_id.

Use the condition START WITH parent_assembly IS NULL to report on all assemblies and their subassemblies.

In a CONNECT BY query, the keyword PRIOR represents an operator that returns a column's value from the parent row. PRIOR is often used to define the recursive relationship, but you may also use PRIOR in SELECT lists, WHERE clauses, or anywhere else that you wish to reference a value from the current row's parent.

WHERE clauses (Oracle)

CONNECT BY queries may have WHERE clauses, but they often do not because the START WITH condition tends to identify the particular tree(s) of interest.

Joins (Oracle)

CONNECT BY queries may involve joins, in which case the following order of operations applies:

1. The join is materialized first, which means that any join predicates are evaluated first.

2. The CONNECT BY processing is applied to the rows returned from the join operation.

3. Any filtering predicates from the WHERE clause are applied to the results of the CONNECT BY operation.

Be careful! Don't write joins that inadvertently eliminate nodes from the hierarchy you are querying.

Hierarchical sorts (Oracle)

Oracle's CONNECT BY syntax implies an ordering in which each parent node is followed by its immediate children, with each child followed by its own immediate children, and so on. It's rare to write a standard ORDER BY clause into a CONNECT BY query because the resulting sort destroys the hierarchical ordering of the data. However, beginning in Oracle9*i* you can use the new ORDER SIBLINGS BY clause to sort each level independently without destroying the hierarchy:

```
SELECT assembly_id, assembly_name, parent_assembly
FROM bill_of_materials
```

```
START WITH assembly_id = 100
CONNECT BY parent_assembly = PRIOR assembly_id
ORDER SIBLINGS BY assembly_name;
```

```
ASSEMBLY_ID ASSEMBLY_NAME              PARENT_ASSEMBLY
----------- ----------------------    ---------------
        100 Automobile
        120 Body                                  100
        122 Left Door                             120
        139 Left Door Frame                       122
        140 Left Window                           122
        141 Lock                                  122
        123 Right Door                            120
        144 Lock                                  123
        142 Right Door Frame                      123
        143 Right Window                          123
        121 Roof                                  120
```

Look carefully at these results; you'll see that at the first level underneath Automobile you have Body followed by Roof. Underneath Body, you have Left Door and Right Door. Each level in the hierarchy is sorted independently, yet each parent is still followed by its immediate children—the hierarchy remains intact.

Loops in hierarchical data (Oracle)

Hierarchical data can sometimes be malformed in that a row's child may also be that row's parent or ancestor. Such a situation leads to a *loop*. To detect such problems, add NOCYCLE to your CONNECT BY clause, and the CONNECT_BY_ISCYCLE pseudocolumn to your SELECT list:

```
SELECT RPAD(' ', 2*(LEVEL-1))
       || assembly_name assembly_name,
       quantity, CONNECT_BY_ISCYCLE
FROM bill_of_materials
START WITH assembly_id = 100
CONNECT BY NOCYCLE parent_assembly = PRIOR assembly_id;
```

NOCYCLE prevents Oracle from following recursive loops in the data. CONNECT_BY_ISCYCLE returns 1 for any row having a child that is also a parent or ancestor.

To create a loop in the sample data for this book, execute the following statement:

```
UPDATE bill_of_materials
SET parent_assembly = 113
WHERE assembly_id=100;
```

Do not COMMIT this statement. Execute the preceding SELECT to see the one row with a problem child, and then ROLLBACK to restore your data to its original state.

CONNECT BY functions and operators (Oracle)

Oracle implements a number of helpful functions and operators to use in writing CONNECT BY queries:

CONNECT_BY_ISCYCLE
> Returns 1 when a row's child is also its ancestor; otherwise returns 0. Use with CONNECT BY NOCYCLE. (Oracle Database 10g and higher)

CONNECT_BY_ISLEAF
> Returns 1 for leaf rows, 0 for rows having children. (Oracle Database 10g and higher)

CONNECT_BY_ROOT(*column*) or CONNECT_BY_ROOT *column*
> Returns a value from the root row. See PRIOR. (Oracle Database 10g and higher)

LEVEL
> Returns 0 for the root node of a hierarchy, 1 for nodes just below the root, 2 for the next level of nodes, and so forth. LEVEL is commonly used to indent hierarchical results. For example, the incantation RPAD(' ', 2*(LEVEL-1)) || *first_column* may be used to indent each level two spaces underneath the other.

PRIOR(*column*) or PRIOR *column*
> Returns a value from a row's parent. See CONNECT_BY_ROOT.

SYS_CONNECT_BY_PATH (column, delimiter)

Returns a concatenated list of *column* values in the path from the root to the current node. Each column value is preceded by a *delimiter*. Add SYS_CONNECT_BY_PATH(assembly_id, '/') to the SELECT list in the preceding section, and you'll get results such as /100, /100/120, and /100/120/122. (Oracle9*i* and higher)

Inserting Data

Use the INSERT statement to insert new rows into a table. You can insert one row or the results of a subquery.

Single-Row Inserts

Use the following form of INSERT to add one row to a table:

```
INSERT INTO table
(column, column, column...)
VALUES (value, value, value...)
```

The following example adds an artist to the artist table. The values in the VALUES clause correspond to the columns listed after the table name:

```
INSERT INTO artist (website, name)
VALUES ('www.gennick.com/andrew/',
        'Andrew Sears');
```

Any columns you omit from an INSERT statement take on their default values specified at table-creation time, with the default default value being NULL:

```
INSERT INTO artist (name)
VALUES ('Jeff Gennick');
```

Use the DEFAULT keyword to explicitly specify that a column should take on its default value:

```
INSERT INTO artist (name, website)
VALUES ('Anna Sears', DEFAULT);
```

Use the NULL keyword to explicitly insert a NULL value into a column that might otherwise default to a non-NULL value:

```
INSERT INTO artist (name, website)
VALUES ('Aaron Sears', NULL);
```

If your VALUES list contains a value for each column in the table in the order specified at table creation, you can omit the column list:

```
INSERT INTO artist
VALUES ('Ted Rexstrew', NULL);
```

For anything other than an ad-hoc insert (in other words, for queries you embed in your scripts and programs), it's safer to specify a list of columns. Otherwise, such queries will fail the moment a new column is added to the target table.

Insert Targets

While the target of an INSERT is often a table, you can also insert into a view or a subquery:

```
INSERT INTO (SELECT * FROM cd)
   (cd_id, title, price)
   VALUES (6, 'Andrews Pirated Legends', 9.95);
```

Oracle can insert into views and subqueries (think of such subqueries as *inline views*). SQL Server and DB2 support inserts into views, but not into subqueries. MySQL supports neither views, nor inserts into subqueries.

Subquery Inserts

Using a subquery, it's possible to insert a number of rows at one time using the following form:

```
INSERT INTO table (column, column ...)
   (SELECT expression, expression ...
    FROM source_table
    ...)
```

The SELECT statement in this form of INSERT must return an expression corresponding to each column listed after the target table. You can sometimes get away without the parentheses surrounding the subquery, but it's safer to include them. The subquery can be any valid SELECT statement. It may return zero, one, or many rows.

Here's an example of a multi-row insert:

```
INSERT INTO song (cd_id, track, artist)
    (SELECT 6, track, 'Andrew Sears'
    FROM song
    WHERE cd_id=1);
```

This INSERT creates a list of songs for CD #6 based on the list from CD #1, but changes the artist name.

Direct-Path Inserts (Oracle)

Oracle supports so-called *direct-path inserts*, which are especially useful for increasing performance when inserting rows from a subquery. Use the APPEND hint to get such an insert:

```
INSERT /*+ APPEND */
    INTO song (cd_id, track, artist)
    (SELECT 6, track, 'Andrew Sears'
    FROM song
    WHERE cd_id=1);
```

Direct-path inserts bypass the database buffer cache. Data is written directly to datafiles, and above the high-water mark. Existing free space is not reused.

Several restrictions apply to direct-path inserts (see the section on INSERT in Oracle's *SQL Reference* for details). If you violate a restriction, you'll receive an error.

RETURNing Inserted Values (Oracle)

In some applications it's helpful to return one or more of the values just inserted. For example, given a table with an automatically incrementing primary key, you might want to find out what key value was assigned to the row you just inserted.

Rather than SELECT the row back, just use the RETURNING clause. Following is an example that will work in Oracle SQL*Plus:

```
VARIABLE url VARCHAR2(25);

INSERT INTO artist (name)
    VALUES ('Donna Gennick')
    RETURNING website INTO :url;
```

The VARIABLE command is a SQL*Plus command to create a bind variable. This example returns one column. You can return more than one by simply separating column names and result variables using commas:

```
RETURNING col1, col2 ... INTO var1, var2...
```

SQL Server, DB2, and MySQL do not support the RETURNING clause.

Multi-Table Inserts (Oracle)

Using Oracle, you can issue INSERTs that affect multiple tables at once. You can insert the results of a subquery unconditionally into several tables, or you can write predicates that control which rows are inserted into which table. If you choose to write predicates, you can choose whether evaluation stops with one success, or whether a row is considered for insertion into more than one table.

Unconditional multi-table insert (Oracle)

Use INSERT ALL to insert the results of a subquery into more than one target table:

```
INSERT ALL
    INTO attraction_urls (id, url)
    VALUES (attraction_id,
            'http://' || attraction_url)
    INTO attraction_names (id, name)
    VALUES (attraction_id, UPPER(attraction_name))
    SELECT attraction_id, attraction_url,
           attraction_name
    FROM attraction;
```

This INSERT splits URLs and names into two separate tables. Different data is inserted into each table, but all data comes from the subquery. Each row returned by the subquery results in two new rows, one in each table.

Conditional multi-table insert (Oracle)

Use WHEN clauses to conditionally insert into multiple tables. The following example places attractions into different tables by county (Alger and Marquette counties respectively) based on the cities represented in the example data:

```
INSERT ALL
    WHEN attraction_id = 1 THEN
        INTO alger_attractions
        VALUES (attraction_id, attraction_name,
                attraction_url, government_owned,
                city_id)
    WHEN attraction_id IN (3,16) THEN
        INTO marquette_attractions
        VALUES (attraction_id, attraction_name,
                attraction_url, government_owned,
                city_id)
    ELSE INTO other_attractions
        VALUES (attraction_id, attraction_name,
                attraction_url, government_owned,
                city_id)
    SELECT * FROM attraction;
```

The ELSE clause in this statement causes all rows not meeting any other criteria to be added to the other_attractions table. The ELSE clause is optional; omit it to ignore rows not meeting at least one WHEN condition.

ALL versus FIRST (Oracle)

In a conditional multi-table INSERT, the keyword ALL causes each row returned by the subquery to be evaluated against each WHEN clause. Thus, a row meeting criteria in two clauses can be inserted into more than one table. Use INSERT FIRST to stop evaluating a row after the first matching WHEN clause.

Joining Tables

Joins allow you to combine data from multiple tables into a single result-set row. There are two fundamental types of join: the *inner join* and the *outer join*. There are also two join syntaxes: the newer SQL 1992 syntax, which depends on a JOIN clause (you should use this whenever possible), and an older syntax in which you separate table names using commas (you will often see this in existing code).

The Concept of a Join

I can best explain the concept of a join by beginning with the early, obsolete syntax. To join related rows from two tables, begin by listing two table expressions separated by a comma in your FROM clause. For example, to retrieve a list of government-owned attractions and city names, you could begin by writing:

```
SELECT attraction_name, city_name
FROM city, attraction
WHERE government_owned='Y';
```

```
ATTRACTION_NAME                       CITY_NAME
------------------------------------  ----------------
Pictured Rocks                        Munising
Pictured Rocks                        St. Ignace
Pictured Rocks                        Marquette
...
```

Obviously something is wrong here—the same attraction can't possibly be in all these cities. The "problem" is that the join in this example is a *Cartesian join*, returning all possible combinations of city and attraction. Such a combination is called a *Cartesian product*, and it's rarely the result you want.

Conceptually, all joins begin as a Cartesian product. From there, it's up to you to supply conditions to winnow down the results to only those rows that make sense. Using the older join syntax, you do that winnowing in the WHERE clause:

```
SELECT attraction_name, city_name
FROM city c, attraction a
WHERE government_owned='Y'
AND c.city_id = a.city_id;

ATTRACTION_NAME                     CITY_NAME
----------------------------------- ----------------
Pictured Rocks                      Munising
Valley Spur                         Munising
Mackinac Bridge                     St. Ignace
...
```

These results are much more believable. Notice the following condition in the WHERE clause:

```
AND c.city_id = a.city_id;
```

This condition is often referred to as a *join condition*. It links desired rows from two tables together. In this case, the comma-delimited list of tables in the FROM clause generates a Cartesian product. That Cartesian product feeds into the WHERE clause processing, which throws away all the rows you don't want in the final result set.

TIP

If your database supports the JOIN keyword, you should use the newer SQL 1992 join syntax described in the remainder of this section on joins.

The process I've just described is purely conceptual—databases will rarely or never form a Cartesian product when executing a join. But thinking in these conceptual terms will help you write correct join queries and help you understand the results from those queries. However the join operation is optimized, join results must in the end match the conceptual results. Don't get bogged down in how your database executes a join. Work conceptually towards the correct results, and worry about how the database actually executes the join only after it's generating the results you want.

Cross Joins

The ANSI standard uses the term *cross join* to describe a Cartesian product. Generate such a cross join as follows:

```
SELECT *
FROM city CROSS JOIN attraction;
```

The keywords CROSS JOIN are from the newer, SQL 1992 join syntax. Using that syntax, it's impossible to inadvertently generate a Cartesian product by omitting the join conditions. You must explicitly ask for such results, which are rarely (if ever) useful.

Inner Joins

An *inner join* relates each row in one table to one or more corresponding rows in another table. Each result row from an inner join represents the combination of values from two related rows, one from each of the tables being joined.

SQL 1992 inner join syntax

The following example illustrates the SQL 1992 inner join syntax. The city table is joined to the attraction table so that each attraction can be listed in its corresponding city.

```
SELECT c.city_name, a.attraction_name
FROM city c INNER JOIN attraction a
    ON c.city_id = a.city_id;

CITY_NAME          ATTRACTION_NAME
----------------   --------------------
Munising           Pictured Rocks
Munising           Valley Spur
Munising           Shipwreck Tours
...
```

The keywords INNER JOIN between the two tables specify that the join should be an inner join. The ON clause specifies the *join condition*, or the condition that must apply in order for two rows to be considered related. Conceptually, as described in the preceding section, a Cartesian product is formed, and the join condition is then applied to winnow out unwanted combinations of rows.

The order of tables in an inner join is irrelevant. The INNER keyword is optional. The following query generates results identical to the previous one:

```
SELECT c.city_name, a.attraction_name
FROM attraction a JOIN city c
    ON c.city_id = a.city_id;
```

A WHERE clause is still valid in join queries. For example, to report on only government-owned tourist attractions, specify:

```
SELECT c.city_name, a.attraction_name
FROM attraction a JOIN city c
    ON c.city_id = a.city_id
WHERE a.government_owned='Y';
```

Conceptually, the join results are materialized first, and the WHERE clause then restricts the results to those joined rows that satisfy the WHERE conditions.

Join precedence and parentheses

Multiple joins are processed from left to right. For example, the following query joins county to city, and then joins those results to attraction:

```
SELECT *
FROM county y JOIN city c
    ON y.county_id = c.county_id
    JOIN attraction a
    ON c.city_id = a.city_id;
```

You can use parentheses to explicitly specify the order of operations. The following query is semantically equivalent to the first:

```
SELECT *
FROM (county y JOIN city c
    ON y.county_id = c.county_id)
    JOIN attraction a
    ON c.city_id = a.city_id;
```

To reverse the join order, joining `attraction` to `city` *before* joining those results to `county`, rearrange the query as follows. Notice the movement of the ON clause for the join to county; it now comes at the end of the query:

```
SELECT *
FROM county y JOIN (city c
     JOIN attraction a
     ON c.city_id = a.city_id)
     ON y.county_id = c.county_id;
```

Parentheses and the order of join operations might become important when working with outer joins. When working strictly with inner joins, moving the parentheses around should not affect the final results because, by definition, each final result row from any number of inner join operations must represent one row from each table involved.

The USING clause

When the columns defining a join between two tables are identically named, and when the join condition would be an equality condition requiring that each set of identically named columns contain the same value (an *equi-join*), you can write the join somewhat more simply by replacing the ON clause with the USING clause. Note that neither SQL Server nor DB2 supports the USING clause.

```
SELECT c.city_name, a.attraction_name
FROM attraction a JOIN city c
     USING (city_id)
WHERE a.government_owned='Y';
```

This query will work in MySQL but not in Oracle. In Oracle there is a subtle but important semantic difference between the ON and the USING versions of a join. The ON version of this join will return two `city_id` columns, one from each of the joined tables: `c.city_id` and `a.city_id`. The USING version of the join, however, will return only a single `city_id` column, which you may *not* qualify with an alias:

```
SELECT c.city_id, a.city_id, a.attraction_name
FROM attraction a JOIN city c
```

```
    USING (city_id);

ERROR at line 1:
ORA-25154: column part of USING clause cannot have
qualifier

SELECT city_id, a.attraction_name
FROM attraction a JOIN city c
    USING (city_id);

  CITY_ID ATTRACTION_NAME
---------- -------------------
         1 Pictured Rocks
         1 Valley Spur
         1 Shipwreck Tours
```

I have no idea why this semantic difference exists in Oracle between the USING and ON forms of a join. MySQL, even with the USING clause, still returns both a c.city_id value and an a.city_id value.

Natural joins

There is yet another shortcut beyond USING. If two tables should be joined based on *all* columns they have in common with the same name, and the join is an equi-join, you may use the NATURAL JOIN keywords without explicitly specifying the join conditions. Neither SQL Server nor DB2 supports NATURAL JOINs.

In Oracle you may not qualify a NATURAL JOIN column with an alias:

```
SELECT city_id, a.attraction_name
FROM attraction a NATURAL JOIN city c;
```

In MySQL, on the other hand, you *must* qualify join columns, even implicit join columns, with aliases:

```
SELECT c.city_id, a.attraction_name
FROM attraction a NATURAL JOIN city c;
```

I don't recommend using NATURAL JOIN, especially in queries that you encapsulate within program code. The simple addition of a column to one table, with a name that happens to match a column in a joined table, can suddenly change the semantics of a NATURAL JOIN query. If you do use NATURAL JOIN, use it only for ad-hoc queries, and even then, be careful!

Non-Equi-Joins

So far, all the joins I've illustrated have been equi-joins, which involve corresponding columns from two tables having the exact same values in two corresponding rows. Equi-joins are probably the most common type of joins, but it is sometimes useful and necessary to write join conditions that are not equality-based. Such joins are sometimes referred to as *non-equi-joins*.

For example, the following join, involving tables from the exposure example, searches for overlap between the period of time a worker is stationed in a given building and the time in which certain chemicals were used within that building:

```
SELECT *
FROM worker_location w
    INNER JOIN building_exposure be
    ON w.building_number = be.building_number
    AND w.begin_date <= be.end_date
    AND w.end_date >= be.begin_date;
```

This simple query doesn't take into account the possibility that any of the date columns could be NULL, but it serves as a good illustration of a join not involving equality conditions. What matters is not whether two dates are equal, but whether one date falls within a range defined by two other dates.

See the section on "NULLs" for a version of this query that accounts for possible NULL dates.

Outer Joins

An *outer join* is one in which each row in the result set does not necessarily have to contain a row from both tables being joined; one or both tables are treated as optional. If you want a join done only when possible, and you want rows back regardless, then use an outer join.

Left outer joins

Use a *left outer join* when you want all rows from one table, regardless of whether corresponding rows exist in the other table. Consider the possibility of an attraction not tied to a city: a row with a NULL city_id exists in the attraction table. You want to list attractions and their cities, but you want to list *all* attractions, even when no corresponding city row exists. You can do that using a left outer join:

```
SELECT c.city_name, a.attraction_name
FROM attraction a LEFT OUTER JOIN city c
    ON c.city_id = a.city_id;

CITY_NAME          ATTRACTION_NAME
----------------   -------------------------
...
Ishpeming          Da Yoopers Tourist Trap
Ishpeming          Ski Hall of Fame
                   Grand Sable Dunes
                   Mount Arvon
                   Wells State Park
```

A left outer join designates the leftmost table as the *required table*. In this case, the leftmost table is the attraction table. Thus, each row in the final result from the query must correspond to a row from the attraction table. The city table is the *optional table*. If a city row exists that corresponds to an attraction, the result is the same as from an inner join: a row with values from both tables. If no city row corresponds to an attraction, a row is returned for the attraction, but with NULLs in place of all the city table values.

TIP

The USING and NATURAL clauses, as well as parentheses, may be used with outer joins in the same way they are used with inner joins.

In this section's example, the final three city names are NULL, indicating either that no city rows correspond to those attractions, or that any corresponding rows contain NULL for the city name.

Interpreting NULLs in an outer join

Think carefully when writing outer joins that include tests for NULLity. The following query attempts to list all government-owned attractions while also including cities for which no attractions exist:

```
SELECT attraction_name, city_name
FROM city c LEFT OUTER JOIN attraction a
   ON c.city_id = a.city_id
WHERE a.government_owned = 'Y'
   OR a.government_owned IS NULL;
```

This query is valid only if you have a NOT NULL constraint on the government_owned column in the attraction table. Otherwise, you should use the following, safer query:

```
SELECT attraction_name, city_name
FROM city c LEFT OUTER JOIN attraction a
   ON c.city_id = a.city_id
WHERE (a.government_owned = 'Y'
      OR a.city_id IS NULL);
```

The key to success here is that, because a.city_id is a primary key column and such columns cannot be null, a.city_id IS NULL is a reliable indicator that the row in question is the result of the outer join, and contains no attraction information.

Right outer joins

Semantically, a *right outer join* is the same as a left outer join. The difference is that the required table is the rightmost table, the second table to be listed. For example:

```
SELECT c.city_name, a.attraction_name
FROM city c RIGHT OUTER JOIN attraction a
ON c.city_id = a.city_id;
```

This query is semantically the same as the left outer join in the preceding section: the attraction table is still the required table, and the city table is still the optional table. The only difference is the order in which those tables are listed in the FROM clause.

TIP

To avoid confusion between left and right, many SQL programmers write all such joins as LEFT OUTER JOINs.

Full outer joins

Sometimes you want an outer join in which both tables are optional. Such a join is a *full outer join*, and is not supported by MySQL. You can write one as follows:

```
SELECT c.city_name, a.attraction_name
FROM attraction a FULL OUTER JOIN city c
    ON c.city_id = a.city_id;
```

```
CITY_NAME          ATTRACTION_NAME
----------------   ------------------------
Ishpeming          Da Yoopers Tourist Trap
Ishpeming          Ski Hall of Fame
                   Grand Sable Dunes
                   Mount Arvon
                   Wells State Park
Vulcan
Carbondale
Newberry

Brimley
```

This query returns attractions without cities and cities without attractions, all in addition to the standard, inner join results of cities and their corresponding attractions.

Vendor-specific outer join syntax

In the past, database vendors have developed different ways to write outer joins. In Oracle, you used to identify the

---

optional table by adding the suffix (+) to the optional table's column reference in all of the join conditions for the given join. The following query lists all attractions, and also any cities having no attractions:

```
SELECT attraction_name, city_name
FROM city c, attraction a
WHERE c.city_id = a.city_id (+);
```

Reversing the order of the columns in the predicate gives the same result. The key is the location of the (+) operator:

```
SELECT attraction_name, city_name
FROM city c, attraction a
WHERE a.city_id (+) = c.city_id;
```

Older versions of SQL Server supported the use of *= and =* in equality conditions to designate left and right outer joins respectively. For example:

```
SELECT attraction_name, city_name
FROM city c, attraction a
WHERE a.city_id *= c.city_id;
```

Oracle and SQL Server still support these syntaxes, but only for backward compatibility with existing code. Don't use them for new code.

TIP

Your queries will be much easier to understand and debug if you write all joins using the ANSI-standard JOIN clause.

Literals

All databases make provision for embedding literal values in SQL statements. Text and numeric literals are usually quite simple, but there are some nuances to be aware of. Date and time literals tend to be more complex.

Text Literals

The ANSI standard for text literals is to enclose such literals within single quotes:

```
'This is a text literal'
```

Use a double quote when you need to embed a quote within a string:

```
'Isn''t SQL fun?'
```

SQL will treat the doubled quotes as a single quote within the literal:

```
Isn't SQL fun?
```

Prefix a text literal with N or n to generate a literal using the national character set (ANSI and Oracle) or Unicode (SQL Server):

```
N'This is a national character set literal'
n'And so is this'
```

DB2 8.1 does not support this syntax, and SQL Server 8 recognizes only uppercase N.

Oracle Database 10g allows you to specify alternative quoting delimiters, which are always two characters and always include leading and trailing single quotes. For example, to use '[and]' as delimiters, specify:

```
Q'[This isn't as bad as it looks]'
q'[This isn't as bad as it looks]'
```

The (, [, and { characters are special cases in that their corresponding closing delimiters must be),], and } respectively. Otherwise, use the same character to close the string as to open it:

```
Q'|This string is delimited by vertical bars|'
```

You can't use space, tab, or return characters to delimit a string in this manner.

Finally, MySQL allows you to include, in string literals, the escape sequences shown in Table 10.

Table 10. MySQL string literal escape sequences

Escape	Description
\0	NUL character (ASCII zero)
\'	Single quote
\"	Double quote
\b	Backspace
\n	Newline
\r	Carriage return
\t	Tab
\z	ASCII 26, or the Ctrl-Z character
\\	Backslash
\%	Percent sign
_	Underscore

Numeric Literals

Numeric literals follow standard conventions for writing numbers:

```
123    123.45    +123    -123.45
```

Numbers written without a decimal point are generally treated as integers. Oracle allows for a trailing F or D to indicate FLOAT or DOUBLE respectively:

```
123D    123.45F    +123d    -123.45f
```

You can also use scientific notation to write floating-point constants:

```
123.45E+23    123.45e-23
```

These literals are interpreted as 123.45×10^{23} and 123.45×10^{-23} (i.e., $123.45 \div 10^{23}$) respectively.

Datetime Literals

ANSI SQL defines the following formats for date, time, and timestamp literals, with hours being according to a 24-hour clock:

```
DATE 'yyyy-mm-dd'
TIME 'hh:mi:ss [{+|-}hh:mi]'
TIMESTAMP 'yyyy-mm-dd hh:mi:ss [{+|-}hh:mi]'
```

For example, the following refer to 19-Dec-2003, 8:00 P.M., and 8:00 P.M. U.S. Eastern Standard Time on 19-Dec-2003:

```
DATE '2003-12-19'
TIME '20:00:00'
TIMESTAMP '2003-12-19 20:00:00 -5:00'
```

These literal formats are supported in Oracle9*i* and higher and in MySQL, but not in SQL Server and DB2.

Datetime Interval Literals

ANSI SQL defines the following formats for INTERVAL YEAR TO MONTH literals:

```
INTERVAL 'year-month' YEAR TO MONTH
INTERVAL 'year' YEAR
INTERVAL 'month' MONTH
```

Oracle9*i* and higher support these formats, also allowing you to specify a precision for the year, which otherwise defaults to two digits:

```
INTERVAL '42-1' YEAR TO MONTH
INTERVAL '1042' YEAR(4)
```

Similarly, ANSI SQL defines the following formats for INTERVAL DAY TO SECOND literals:

```
INTERVAL 'dd hh:mi:ss.ff' DAY TO SECOND
INTERVAL 'hh:mi' HOUR TO MINUTE
INTERVAL 'mi' MINUTE
...
```

For an INTERVAL DAY TO SECOND literal, you can specify any contiguous range of time elements from days to seconds. In Oracle9*i* and higher, days (*dd*) and fractional seconds (*ff*) both default to two digits of precision.

Neither SQL Server nor MySQL supports the ANSI/ISO interval literal syntax.

Merging Data

Beginning with Oracle8*i*, Oracle supports the MERGE statement that is part of the SQL 2003 standard. MERGE either updates or inserts rows, depending on whether they already exist. The basic syntax is:

```
MERGE INTO table alias
USING datasource ON (exists_test)
WHEN MATCHED THEN UPDATE
    SET column = value, column = value ...
WHEN NOT MATCHED THEN INSERT
    (column, column, ...)
    VALUES (value, value, ...)

datasource ::= {table|view|(subquery)}
```

For example, to merge potentially new county rows into the county table, specify:

```
MERGE INTO county c
USING (SELECT * FROM new_counties) nc
    ON (c.county_id = nc.county_id)
WHEN MATCHED THEN UPDATE
    SET c.county_name = nc.county_name,
        c.state = nc.state
WHEN NOT MATCHED THEN INSERT
    (county_id, county_name, state)
    VALUES (nc.county_id, nc.county_name, nc.state);
```

You can place WHERE conditions on both the UPDATE and INSERT operations. You can also specify rows to be DELETEd following an UPDATE operation:

```
MERGE INTO county c
USING (SELECT * FROM new_counties) nc
    ON (c.county_id = nc.county_id)
WHEN MATCHED THEN UPDATE
```

```
        SET c.county_name = nc.county_name,
            c.state = nc.state
        WHERE c.county_name <> nc.county_name
        DELETE WHERE c.county_id = 18
    WHEN NOT MATCHED THEN INSERT
        (county_id, county_name, state)
        VALUES (nc.county_id, nc.county_name, nc.state)
        WHERE nc.county_name IS NOT NULL;
```

This statement restricts updates to name changes, arbitrarily deletes any *updated* record with a post-update ID of 18, and inserts new records only with non-NULL names.

NOTE

DELETE WHERE is a post-update deletion. Rows not updated by the MERGE statement are not candidates for deletion.

NULLs

When writing SQL, it's critical to understand NULLs and three-valued logic. With few exceptions, the result of any expression involving a NULL will itself be NULL, and this has ramifications for any expression (comparison or otherwise) that you write.

Predicates for NULLs

You cannot compare NULLs to any other value using the standard comparison operators. For example, the following query will *not* return all rows from the city table:

```
SELECT * FROM city
WHERE city_name = 'Munising'
   OR city_name <> 'Munising';
```

You'd think that any given city name would either be Munising or not be Munising, but such is not the case. A NULL city name is not Munising, nor is it not *not* Munising.

ANSI/ISO SQL provides the IS NULL and IS NOT NULL predicates to detect the presence or absence of NULL values. To find all cities other than Munising, including those whose names are NULL, specify:

```
SELECT * FROM city
WHERE city_name <> 'Munising'
    OR city_name IS NULL;
```

The following more complex example is a NULL-safe version of a query shown earlier in "Non-Equi-Joins." This version of the query allows end dates to be NULL, and interprets a NULL end date as an indication that the exposure condition is ongoing:

```
SELECT *
FROM worker_location w
    INNER JOIN building_exposure be
    ON w.building_number = be.building_number
    AND (w.begin_date <= be.end_date
        OR be.end_date IS NULL)
    AND (w.end_date >= be.begin_date
        OR w.end_date IS NULL);
```

Similarly, you can use IS NOT NULL to explicitly match non-NULL values.

NOTE

In Oracle, a LOB (large object) column may be either NULL or empty. A NULL LOB column has no locator, and hence no data. An empty LOB has a locator, but still no data.

Using CASE with NULLs

CASE expressions can sometimes be helpful when working with potentially NULL data. For example, to ensure you always get a non-NULL city name, specify:

```
SELECT city_id,
       CASE WHEN city_name IS NOT NULL THEN city_name
       ELSE '***No Name***' END
FROM city;
```

Most databases also provide functions to do this same type of thing more succinctly.

Functions for NULLs (Oracle)

Oracle's DECODE, COALESCE, NVL, and NVL2 functions are all helpful when dealing with potentially NULL data.

COALESCE was introduced in Oracle9*i* and is part of SQL 1999. It takes an arbitrary list of arguments and returns the first non-NULL value it encounters:

```
SELECT city_id, COALESCE(city_name, '***No Name***')
FROM city;
```

You can provide any number of arguments, and you should ensure that at least one will be non-NULL. If all arguments are NULL, COALESCE returns NULL.

NVL is equivalent to COALESCE with only two arguments:

```
SELECT city_id, NVL(city_name, '***No Name***')
FROM city;
```

NVL2 returns one of two values, depending on whether the first is NULL:

```
SELECT city_id,
       NVL2(city_name, city_name, '***No Name***')
FROM city;
```

DECODE is equivalent to an inline IF statement, and provides yet another way of dealing with NULLs:

```
SELECT city_id,
       DECODE(city_name,
              NULL, '***No Name***',
              'Munising','Jonathan''s Home',
              city_name)
FROM city;
```

In this example, city_name is the input value. If the input value is NULL (second argument), then the third argument is returned. If the input value is 'Munising' (fourth argument), then the fifth argument is returned. Otherwise, the final argument is returned. DECODE supports any number of input/result pairs.

Functions for NULLs (DB2)

DB2 supports the ANSI/ISO COALESCE function, as described earlier for Oracle.

DB2 also supports the NULLIF function, which returns NULL whenever the two input values are the same:

```
SELECT NULLIF(city_name,'Munising')...
```

If city_name = 'Munising', this NULLIF call returns NULL; otherwise, it returns the value of city_name.

Functions for NULLs (SQL Server)

SQL Server supports the ANSI/ISO COALESCE function, as described earlier for Oracle.

SQL Server also supports a setting known as ANSI_NULLS, which affects the behavior of = and <> predicates that compare to NULL:

```
...WHERE city_name = NULL
...WHERE city_name <> NULL
```

By default, neither of these predicates will ever match any rows. However, issue the command SET ANSI_NULLS OFF, and you can use = NULL and <> NULL to search for NULL or NOT NULL values respectively.

Functions for NULLs (MySQL)

With MySQL, use IFNULL to return an alternate value for a potentially NULL input value. For example:

```
SELECT city_id,
       IFNULL(city_name, '***No Name***')
FROM city;
```

Like DB2, MySQL supports NULLIF to return NULL whenever two input values are the same:

```
SELECT NULLIF(city_name,'Munising')...
```

You can also use the IF function to return one of two values, depending on whether an expression is TRUE:

```
SELECT city_id,
       IF(city_name IS NULL,
          '***No Name***', city_name)
FROM city;
```

You'd normally use a comparison expression to generate the Boolean TRUE/FALSE value for the first argument. If the expression evaluates to TRUE, the value from the second argument is returned. Otherwise, if the expression evaluates to FALSE or NULL, the third argument's value is returned.

Predicates

Predicates are conditions you write in the WHERE clause (and the HAVING clause) of a SQL statement that determine the rows affected by, or returned by, that statement. For example:

```
SELECT title
FROM song
WHERE artist = 'Carl Behrend';
```

In this example, artist = 'Carl Behrend' is a predicate, specifying that the query is to return only songs performed by Carl. Table 11 lists the available comparison operators. Some operators, such as IN and EXISTS, are more fully described in upcoming subsections. Regular-expression operators are described in the later section "Regular Expressions."

Table 11. Comparison operators

Operator	Description
!=, <>, ^=	Tests for inequality. Only Oracle supports ^=. DB2 supports only <>.
<	Tests for less-than.
<=	Tests for less-than or equal-to.
<=>	NULL-safe test for equality. Supported only by MySQL.
=	Tests for equality.
>	Tests for greater-than.
>=	Tests for greater-than or equal-to.
BETWEEN	Tests whether a value lies within a given range.
EXISTS	Tests whether rows exist matching conditions you specify.
IN	Tests whether a value is contained in a set of values you specify or that are returned by a subquery.
IS [NOT] NULL	Tests for nullity.
LIKE	Tests whether a value matches a pattern.
REGEXP, RLIKE	Regular-expression comparison operator; supported only by MySQL.
REGEXP_LIKE	Tests whether a value matches the pattern described by a regular expression. Supported only by Oracle.

Be sure to read the earlier section "NULLs," which describes the operators you can use to test for NULL values in a WHERE or HAVING clause.

Group Comparison Predicates

You can use the keywords ANY, SOME, or ALL with the simple comparison operators from Table 11 (those listed before BETWEEN) to compare a single value to a set of values:

```
SELECT title
FROM song
WHERE cd_id = ANY (2, 5);
```

Or:

```
SELECT title
FROM song
WHERE cd_id = ANY
   (SELECT cd_id
    FROM cd
    WHERE price <= 10);
```

MySQL does not support the first form, in which ANY is used to compare to an explicit list of values.

ANY specifies that the condition should be true for at least one value from the set. SOME is a synonym for ANY. Use ALL when you want the condition to be true for *all* values in the set.

Multiple Values on the Left (Oracle)

Oracle lets you specify multiple values on the left side of a comparison. For example, to find all songs matching the length of the longest song on their respective CDs, specify:

```
SELECT cd_id, playing_time, title
FROM song s1
WHERE (cd_id, playing_time)
   = (SELECT cd_id, MAX(playing_time)
      FROM song s2
      WHERE s1.cd_id = s2.cd_id);
```

When using just a simple comparison operator, as in this case, the subquery must return one row.

Using the ANY, SOME, or ALL keyword, you can specify multiple sets of values:

```
SELECT cd_id, playing_time, title
FROM song
WHERE (cd_id, playing_time) = ANY ((3,285), (3,313));
```

You can also use a subquery that returns one or more sets of values:

```
SELECT cd_id, playing_time, title
FROM song
WHERE (cd_id, playing_time)
```

```
        = ANY(SELECT cd_id, MAX(playing_time)
              FROM song
              GROUP BY cd_id);
```

This query also returns all songs matching the length of the longest song on their respective CDs. This time, the subquery is non-correlated, and returns the list of all candidate playing times in one go.

EXISTS Predicates

Use EXISTS and NOT EXISTS to test for the existence of rows matching a set of conditions that you specify. For example, to find all CDs containing at least one song performed by Rondi Olson, specify:

```
SELECT cd_id, title
FROM cd
WHERE EXISTS (SELECT * FROM song
              WHERE cd.cd_id = song.cd_id
                AND song.artist = 'Rondi Olson');
```

Use NOT EXISTS in this same query to find all CDs containing no songs performed by Rondi.

Subqueries used in EXISTS predicates should usually be correlated. In this case, the subquery looks at all songs on the current CD from the cd table.

IN Predicates

Use IN to test whether a value falls within a set of values. You can enumerate that set as a list of literal values, or you can return the set as the result from a subquery. The following example specifies a set of literal values:

```
SELECT cd_id, track, title
FROM song
WHERE cd_id IN (1,3)
ORDER BY cd_id, track;
```

This next example uses a subquery, and is a restatement of the EXISTS query from the preceding section that returns a list of CDs containing songs performed by Rondi Olson:

```
SELECT cd_id, title
FROM cd
WHERE cd_id IN (SELECT cd_id FROM song
                WHERE artist ='Rondi Olson');
```

Watch out for NULLs! If the subquery you use with an IN predicate returns a NULL value for even one row in the set, then the result of the IN (or NOT IN) operation will never be true. Rather, it will always be NULL, and your query won't function as you expect.

BETWEEN Predicates

Use BETWEEN to see whether a value falls in a given range. For example:

```
SELECT title
FROM song
WHERE playing_time BETWEEN 280 AND 300;
```

Any BETWEEN predicate can easily be expressed using the <= and >= operators:

```
SELECT title
FROM song
WHERE playing_time >= 280
  AND playing_time <= 300;
```

When writing BETWEEN predicates, always list the least value first.

LIKE Predicates

The ANSI/ISO LIKE and NOT LIKE predicates give you rudimentary pattern-matching capabilities. You can use the percent (%) and period (.) characters to match any number of characters or any one character, respectively. For example, to find all songs containing the word "Ship" in the title, specify:

```
SELECT title
FROM song
WHERE title LIKE '%Ship%';
```

Use NOT LIKE to find all songs without "Ship" in the title.

In SQL Server, use an underscore (_) rather than a period to find any single character.

Oracle and DB2 support syntax that lets you specify an escape character you can use when you want to use the pattern-matching characters literally. For example, to find all songs without a percent in their titles, specify:

```
SELECT title
FROM song
WHERE title NOT LIKE '%\%%' ESCAPE '\';
```

Unlike Oracle and DB2, MySQL recognizes the backslash (\) as an escape character by default:

```
SELECT title
FROM song
WHERE title NOT LIKE '%\%%';
```

When specifying an escape character in MySQL, remember that the backslash is the string-literal escape character. Thus, to explicitly specify the backslash as the LIKE escape character, you must escape that backslash in the ESCAPE clause:

```
SELECT title
FROM song
WHERE title NOT LIKE '%\%%' ESCAPE '\\';
```

Oracle also implements LIKEC, LIKE2, and LIKE4, which work with Unicode characters, code units, and code points, respectively.

Recursive Queries

See "Hierarchical Queries."

Regular Expressions

Oracle, SQL Server, and MySQL support *regular expressions* (regexes). SQL Server and MySQL support them for string comparison, and Oracle for much more than that. DB2 Version 8.1 does not support regular expressions at all.

Regular Expressions (Oracle)

Oracle Database 10g implements the following regular-expression functions:

```
REGEXP_INSTR(source_string, pattern
            [, position [, occurrence
            [, return_option
            [, match_parameter]]]])

REGEXP_LIKE (source_string, pattern
            [, match_parameter])

REGEXP_REPLACE(source_string, pattern
              [, replace_string
              [, position [, occurrence
              [, match_parameter]]]])

REGEXP_SUBSTR(source_string, pattern
             [, position [, occurrence
             [, match_parameter]]])
```

Parameters are as follows:

source_string

>The string you wish to search.

pattern

>A regular expression describing the text pattern you are searching for. This expression may not exceed 512 bytes in length.

replace_string

>The replacement text. Each occurrence of *pattern* in *source_string* is replaced by *replace_string*, which can

---

use backreferences to refer to values matching subexpressions in the pattern.

position
> The character position at which to begin the search. This defaults to 1, and must be positive.

occurrence
> The occurrence of *pattern* you are interested in finding. This defaults to 1. Specify 2 if you want to find the second occurrence of the pattern, 3 for the third occurrence, and so forth.

return_option
> Specify 0 (the default) to return the pattern's beginning character position. Specify 1 to return the ending character position.

match_parameter
> A set of options in the form of a character string that changes the default manner in which regular-expression pattern matching is performed. You may specify any, all, or none of the following options, in any order:
>
> 'i' Specifies case-insensitive matching.
>
> 'c' Specifies case-sensitive matching.
>
> 'n' Allows the period (.) to match the newline character. (Normally, that is not the case.)
>
> 'm' Causes the caret (^) and dollar sign ($) to match the beginning and ending, respectively, of lines within the source string. Normally, the caret and dollar sign match only the very beginning and the very ending of the source string, regardless of any newline characters within the string.

The NLS_SORT parameter setting determines whether case-sensitive or insensitive matching is done by default.

Table 12 lists the regular-expression metacharacters supported by these functions.

Table 12. Oracle regular-expression metacharacters

Operator	Description
\	Escapes a metacharacter
\1 ... \9	Backreferences an earlier subexpression; the `replace_string` parameter supports from \1 to \500
.	Matches any character
^	Matches beginning-of-line
$	Matches end-of-line
[...]	Matches any of a set of characters
[^...]	Matches any character *not* in a set
[.xx.]	Encloses a collation element
[:class:]	Specifies a character class such as [:digit:], [:alpha:], [:upper:], etc., within a bracket expression
[=chars=]	Specifies an equivalence class
*	Matches zero or more
+	Matches one or more
?	Matches zero or one
{x}, {x,y}, {x,}	Matches x times, from x to y times, or at least x times
|	Delimits alternatives
(...)	Defines a subexpression

Regular Expressions (SQL Server)

SQL Server supports a very limited regular-expression syntax for its version of the LIKE predicate. For example, to find Alger county even if it is misspelled as "Aljer," specify:

```
SELECT *
FROM county
WHERE county_name LIKE 'Al[gj]er';
```

SQL Server does not support quantifiers, alternation, sub-expressions, or backreferences. Table 13 lists the very few metacharacters that SQL Server does support.

Table 13. SQL Server regular-expression metacharacters

Operator	Description
%	Matches any number of characters
_	Matches any character, including newlines
[...]	Matches any of a set of characters
[^...]	Matches any character *not* in a set

Regular Expressions (MySQL)

In MySQL, you can perform regular-expression pattern matching using the REGEXP predicate in a manner similar to LIKE:

```
string REGEXP pattern
```

For example, to search for the pattern "SHIP" at the end of a string, specify:

```
SELECT title
FROM song
WHERE title REGEXP 'SHIP$';
```

MySQL's regular-expression pattern matching is case-insensitive for non-binary strings. Because MySQL recognizes the backslash (\) as an escape character in string literals, you must use a double backslash (\\) to represent a single backslash in any pattern that you write as a literal.

Table 14 lists the regular-expression metacharacters recognized by MySQL.

Table 14. MySQL regular-expression metacharacters

Operator	Description
.	Matches any character, including newlines
^	Matches beginning-of-string

Table 14. MySQL regular-expression metacharacters (continued)

Operator	Description
$	Matches end-of-string
[...]	Matches any of a set of characters
[^...]	Matches any character *not* in a set
[[.*xx*.]]	Matches a collation element
[:*class*:]	Specifies a character class such as [:digit:], [:alpha:], [:upper:], etc., within a bracket expression
[=*chars*=]	Specifies an equivalence class
*	Matches zero or more
+	Matches one or more
?	Matches zero or one
{*x*}, {*x,y*}, {*x,*}	Matches *x* times, from *x* to *y* times, or at least *x* times
|	Delimits alternatives
(...)	Defines a subexpression
[[:<:]]	Matches the beginning of a word
[[:>:]]	Matches the end of a word

Selecting Data

Use a SELECT statement, or *query*, to retrieve data from a database, typically from a table or view or from a combination of tables and views:

```
SELECT expression_list
FROM data_source
WHERE predicates
GROUP BY expression_list
HAVING predicates
ORDER BY expression_list
```

A SELECT statement returns a set of rows and columns known as a *result set*.

DB2 and Oracle support factoring out subqueries using a WITH clause. See "Hierarchical Queries" and "Subqueries" for some examples of this technique.

The SELECT Clause

Each expression in the SELECT clause becomes a column in the result set returned by the query. Expressions may be simple column names, may generate a new value using a column value as input, or may have nothing to do with any columns at all.

Specifying column names

The SELECT clause specifies the individual data elements you want the statement to return. Each item in the expression list translates to one column in the statement's result set. The simple case is to specify a comma-delimited list of one or more column names from the tables listed in the FROM clause:

```
SELECT title, price
FROM cd;
```

The result set for this query will contain the following columns:

```
TITLE                          PRICE
------------------------------ -----
Legends of the Great Lakes     17.95
Nothing Less                      10
More Legends of the Great Lakes 17.95
The Ballad of Seul Choix       17.95
Seeing the Unseen                 10
```

Each column in a result set is given a name. In the simple case shown here, the database column names are used as the result set column names.

Taking shortcuts with the asterisk

To return all columns from a table, you can specify a single asterisk rather than writing out each column name:

```
SELECT *
FROM cd;
```

```
CD_ID TITLE            PRICE ARTIST
------ --------------- ------ ------------
     1 Legends of the  17.95 Carl Behrend
       Great Lakes
     2 Nothing Less    10.00 Rondi Olson
  ...
```

Using the asterisk is a helpful shortcut when executing queries interactively because it can save you a fair bit of typing.
However, it's a risky proposition to use the asterisk in program code because the columns in a table may change over
time, causing your program to fail when more or fewer columns than expected are returned.

Another reason to be explicit when writing programs is that
the asterisk returns all columns to the client, often across a
network. Save bandwidth by returning only the columns you
need.

You can qualify an asterisk, or a column name, with a table
name:

```
SELECT song.*, song.artist
FROM cd, song
WHERE cd.cd_id = song.cd_id;
```

When the asterisk is not the only item in the SELECT list,
you must qualify the asterisk with a table name, as shown in
the preceding statement. (You cannot do this in SQL Server.)

You can retrieve columns redundantly. The following query
returns cd_id twice: once because I listed the column explicitly in the SELECT list (the cd_id expression), and once
because I used cd.* to return all columns from the cd table:

```
SELECT cd_id, cd.*
FROM cd;
```

Strange as this may seem, there are times when I've found it
useful to write such queries.

Writing expressions

You can use column names in expressions. The following statement discounts the price by 10%:

```
SELECT title, price * .90
FROM cd;
```

Not only can you use simple mathematical and other expressions involving operators, all modern databases make an array of functions available. The following SELECT uses the ROUND function to round the discounted price to two decimal places:

```
SELECT title, ROUND(price * .90,2)
FROM cd;
```

It is not necessary for an expression in a SELECT list to refer to any column at all in the table or view from which you are selecting. In Oracle, it's very common to issue queries against a special table known as dual, as in the following query to return the current date and time:

```
SELECT SYSDATE
FROM dual;
```

Your database will evaluate such expressions for each row returned by the query. Oracle's dual table is special in that it holds only one row. Thus, the preceding query will return only one value. If you wish, you could query the cd table and return the current date and time with each row in the result set:

```
SELECT title,
       ROUND(price * .90,2) price,
       SYSDATE
FROM cd;
```

In SQL Server and MySQL, you can return the result of an expression without selecting from a table at all. For example, use the following in SQL Server to get the current time:

```
SELECT getdate( );
```

A SELECT such as this one, in which no table is specified, is the SQL Server/MySQL equivalent of Oracle's SELECT…FROM dual.

Controlling result-set column names

Each column in a SELECT statement's result set is given a name (except in SQL Server, which seems able to return unnamed columns). The following Oracle example shows a query and its attendant result set:

```
SELECT title, ROUND(price * .90,2)
FROM cd;

TITLE                       ROUND(PRICE*.90,2)
-------------------------   ------------------
Legends of the Great Lakes              16.16
Nothing Less                                9
...
```

Result-set column names are important, not only for display purposes as shown here, but because those names are often what you use to access the column values in your program. In a Java program using JDBC, for example, you might get the CD title from the current result-set row as follows:

```
title = rslt.getString("TITLE");
```

Dealing with a column name like TITLE is easy enough, but who wants to write code such as the following?

```
price = rslt.getString("ROUND(PRICE*.90,2)");
```

Yech! Not only is this terribly confusing, but your code will break the minute you give someone a 20% discount instead of the 10% discount shown here.[*] To combat these problems, SQL enables you to specify a name, or *alias*, for each expression in your SELECT list. To specify a column alias,

---

[*] Perhaps for this reason, DB2 generates column names for expressions in the form "1", "2", etc., using digits rather than building complicated names from the expressions themselves.

just place the alias name immediately after the expression, separating the two by at least one space. The following query specifies an alias for both the column and the expression:

```
SELECT title cd_title,
       ROUND(price * .90,2) price
FROM cd;
```

```
CD_TITLE                        PRICE
------------------------- ----------
Legends of the Great Lakes     16.16
Nothing Less                       9
...
```

In a given situation, it may not be important to provide an alias for a simple column name such as TITLE. However, it's very important to use aliases when working with expressions such as the ROUND expression involving the price column. Such aliases insulate your code from inevitable changes to the expressions. In this example, you can plug in any pricing expression, and the resulting column name will always be PRICE.

TIP

You do not need to alias each expression in a SELECT list. You can choose to provide aliases for some expressions or column names, and not for others.

Dealing with case and punctuation in names

By default, SQL is case-insensitive and converts keywords and identifiers (such as table and column names) to uppercase. (Note that MySQL is an exception, and is case-sensitive when it comes to identifiers such as table and column names.) Except in MySQL, you might type in the following:

```
SELECT title CD_Title,
       round(price * .90,2) Price
from cd;
```

but your database will see it as:

```
SELECT TITLE CD_TITLE,
       ROUND(PRICE * .90,2) PRICE
FROM CD;
```

If you must specify an identifier in a case-sensitive manner, you can enclose it within double quotes (MySQL does not support this syntax). The following example uses double quotes to generate mixed-case column aliases. Note that the double quotes also allow for spaces to be made part of the alias names:

```
SELECT title "CD Title",
       ROUND(price * .90,2) "Price"
FROM cd;
```

```
CD Title                          Price
------------------------- ----------
Legends of the Great Lakes   16.16
Nothing Less                      9
...
```

This ability to quote identifiers also enables you to work with column and table names that contain mixed cases, spaces, and other unusual characters. Such names are commonly found in applications written using Microsoft Access. Imagine creating a table using the table and column names shown in the following CREATE TABLE statement:

```
CREATE TABLE "CD Table" (
    "CD ID" NUMBER,
    "CD Title" VARCHAR2(35),
    "Price" NUMBER(4,2),
    "artist" VARCHAR2(15),
    CONSTRAINT cd2_pk
        PRIMARY KEY ("CD ID"),
    CONSTRAINT cd2_unique
        UNIQUE ("CD Title"),
    CONSTRAINT cd2_artist
        FOREIGN KEY ("artist")
        REFERENCES artist);
```

I shudder at the thought of working with such names! However, you can easily query this table by quoting the identifiers:

```
SELECT "CD Title" title,
       ROUND("Price" * .90,2) PRICE
FROM "CD Table";
```

When writing queries like this one, it's a good idea to provide simple, unquoted column aliases. Doing so will help preserve your sanity.

Using subqueries in a SELECT list

Recent database releases allow you to embed a subquery in a SELECT list. Such a subquery must return exactly one row and one column. When writing a subquery into a SELECT list, you must enclose the subquery within parentheses. You should also specify a column alias so the corresponding result-set column has a simple name that you can easily refer to in your code. For example, the following query returns the number of songs on each CD:

```
SELECT title,
       ROUND(price * .90,2) price,
       (SELECT COUNT(*)
        FROM song
        WHERE song.cd_id=cd.cd_id) songs
FROM cd;
```

Subqueries may be correlated or uncorrelated. The subquery in this example happens to be correlated, meaning that it refers to the enclosing table.

Qualifying column names

You can qualify a column name by its table name. This is especially important when writing queries involving multiple tables (see the later section "The FROM Clause") because sometimes two tables will have columns with the same name. To qualify a column name, use dot-notation, as in table_name.column_name. For example:

```
SELECT cd.title,
       ROUND(cd.price * .90,2) price
FROM cd;
```

When you qualify a column name, the table name does not usually become part of the column name. The title column in this example will still be named TITLE. However, because cd.price is embedded within an expression, the cd. will be embedded in the column name that the database generates. This is yet another reason to specify column aliases.

In Oracle, if you qualify a column name by its table name, you may also qualify that table name by its schema name. Likewise, MySQL lets you qualify column names by their database names. Thus, you can write:

```
SELECT sqlpocket.cd.title
FROM sqlpocket.cd;
```

This query returns titles from the cd table in the sqlpocket schema, or, in the case of MySQL, from the sqlpocket database.

ALL and DISTINCT

Use the ALL and DISTINCT keywords to specify whether you want the SELECT operation to eliminate duplicate rows from the result set. (Oracle supports UNIQUE as a synonym for DISTINCT.)

Retrieving all rows

Use the ALL keyword to specify the default behavior for a SELECT statement, which is that the statement returns all rows meeting the conditions specified in the WHERE and HAVING clauses. For example, the following two statements are semantically equivalent, returning the same data:

```
SELECT ALL price
FROM cd;

SELECT price
FROM cd;
```

The ALL keyword must appear immediately following the SELECT keyword.

Eliminating duplicate result set rows

Use the DISTINCT keyword to cause a SELECT statement to eliminate duplicate rows from the result set. For example, to determine the different price points at which you sell CDs, you might begin by issuing a query such as the following:

```
SELECT PRICE
FROM cd;

    PRICE
----------
    17.95
       10
    17.95
    17.95
       10
```

However, this query lists every CD price in the table. Notice that 17.95 is listed three times. If you had 10,000 CDs priced at 17.95, you might not appreciate seeing their price 10,000 times. You really want to know only that you sell one or more CDs at that price, so you need to see the price only once. Use the DISTINCT keyword to accomplish this:

```
SELECT DISTINCT PRICE
FROM cd;

    PRICE
----------
       10
    17.95
```

If you specify DISTINCT with multiple columns, then the combination of those columns must be unique. For example, the following query returns each distinct combination of title and price:

```
SELECT DISTINCT title, price
FROM cd;
```

There are performance implications to using DISTINCT. The database software must eliminate duplicate rows from the result set, which often involves a sort of the data. Elimination of duplicates cannot occur until all rows specified by

WHERE and HAVING have been retrieved; thus, rows cannot be returned to the application as they are found. Instead, the database must materialize the entire result set in temporary storage, sort it, and scan the sorted result set to eliminate duplicates. Only then can the database begin to return query results to the application.

The FROM Clause

Use the FROM clause to specify the source of the data you want to retrieve. The simplest case is to specify a single table or view in the FROM clause of a SELECT statement (remember that MySQL does not support views):

```
SELECT attraction_name
FROM attraction    /* a table */
WHERE city_id=8;

SELECT *
FROM city_attractions    /* a view */
WHERE city_name='Hancock';
```

In Oracle, to facilitate selecting from a table or view owned by another user or in a different schema, you can qualify a table or view name with a schema name using dot-notation:

```
SELECT *
FROM gennick.city_attractions
WHERE city_name='Germfask';
```

This query specifically retrieves from the city_attractions view or table owned by the user gennick.

Table aliases in the FROM clause

You can specify a name, called a *table alias*, for any table expression in a FROM clause. Instead of:

```
SELECT attraction.attraction_name,
       attraction.attraction_url
FROM attraction
WHERE attraction.city_id = 16;
```

you can write:

```
SELECT a.attraction_name, a.attraction_url
FROM attraction a
WHERE a.city_id = 16;
```

Aliases are vital for certain types of queries, for example when you have ambiguous column names as the result of a join or the use of a subquery. The following query returns a list of attractions, and for each attraction shows the number of other attractions in the same city:

```
SELECT a1.attraction_name,
       (SELECT count(*)
        FROM attraction a2
        WHERE a2.city_id = a1.city_id) count
FROM attraction a1;
```

You couldn't write this query without using aliases because the table names are identical. Only with aliases can you differentiate between the two references to the attraction table.

Subqueries in the FROM clause

Subqueries can sometimes be used to good effect in the FROM clause, where they are also known as *inline views*. (Note that MySQL does not support such subqueries.) Such subqueries must be *non-correlated*; in other words, they must not reference columns from the main query. For example, the following query lists all government-owned attractions, and in addition lists each city at least once:

```
SELECT attraction_name, city_name
FROM city c
    LEFT OUTER JOIN
            (SELECT *
             FROM attraction
             WHERE government_owned = 'Y') a
    ON c.city_id = a.city_id;
```

The subquery materializes a temporary table of attractions that are government-owned. That temporary table is then joined to the city table. The join is an outer join, with the result that any city without a government-owned attraction is still listed once in the results.

Collections in the FROM clause (Oracle)

Oracle8 and higher support nested table columns and VARRAY (varying array) columns. You can query from these collection types. For example:

```
SELECT cd.cd_id, s.track, s.title
FROM cd_song cd, TABLE(songs) s
WHERE cd.title='Legends of the Great Lakes';

     CD_ID     TRACK TITLE
---------- ---------- ----------------------------
         1          1 The Christmas Ship
         1          2 Lake Superior Song
         1          3 Captain Bundy's Gospel Ship
...
```

The TABLE function in the FROM clause of this query treats the nested table column songs as a separate table joined to cd_song. The join conditions are implicit: each row in cd_song is joined to all the songs listed in the songs column for that row.

Partitions and subpartitions in the FROM clause (Oracle)

Oracle8 and higher support partitioned tables. You can query from a specific partition, thus returning rows from only that partition, as follows:

```
SELECT *
FROM county PARTITION (michigan);
```

To query from a subpartition, use the SUBPARTITION keyword:

```
SELECT *
FROM county SUBPARTITION (michigan01)
WHERE county_id = 1;
```

Flashback queries (Oracle)

New in Oracle9*i* Release 2 is the flashback clause, enabling you to query against a past state of the database. See the earlier, top-level section "Flashback Queries (Oracle)" for more on this topic.

The WHERE Clause

Use the WHERE clause to restrict query results to only those rows of interest. For example, the following query brings back a complete list of tourist attractions:

```
SELECT attraction_name
FROM attraction;
```

Rarely will you want all rows from a table. More often, you'll want rows matching specific criteria. The following example retrieves only government-owned attractions near the city of Munising:

```
SELECT attraction_name
FROM attraction
WHERE government_owned='Y'
   AND city_id IN (
       SELECT city_id FROM city
       WHERE city_name='Munising');
```

This query uses an equality predicate (=) to identify government-owned facilities, and an IN predicate (IN) to identify sites in Munising. See the "Predicates" section for a list of predicates that you can use in the WHERE clause.

Join conditions also serve to restrict data returned by a query. See the "Joining Tables" section for more on this.

The GROUP BY Clause

See "Grouping and Summarizing."

The HAVING Clause

See "Grouping and Summarizing."

The ORDER BY Clause

Use ORDER BY to specify how you want results to be sorted. For example, to return a list of attractions sorted by city name, and within the city by attraction name, specify:

```
SELECT c.city_name, a.attraction_name
FROM attraction a INNER JOIN city c
    ON a.city_id = c.city_id
ORDER BY c.city_name, a.attraction_name;
```

The default sort is an ascending sort. You can use the keywords ASCENDING and DESCENDING, which you'll usually want to abbreviate to ASC and DESC, to control the sort that's done on each column. The following example is similar to the previous one except that within a city all sites owned by the government are listed first:

```
SELECT c.city_name, a.attraction_name
FROM attraction a INNER JOIN city c
    ON a.city_id = c.city_id
ORDER BY c.city_name,
         a.government_owned DESC,
         a.attraction_name ASC;
```

This example also shows that you can sort on columns (in this case, government_owned) that are not in your SELECT list.

You can get quite creative with ORDER BY, even to the point of sorting by the results of a subquery:

```
SELECT c.city_name, a.attraction_name
FROM attraction a INNER JOIN city c
    ON a.city_id = c.city_id
ORDER BY (SELECT COUNT(*)
           FROM attraction a2
          WHERE a2.city_id = a.city_id) DESC,
         c.city_name,
         a.government_owned DESC,
         a.attraction_name ASC;
```

The ORDER BY clause in this query uses a descending sort on the results of a *correlated* subquery (i.e., one that references a column from the main query) to list first those cities with the greatest number of tourist attractions.

Subqueries

Subqueries may be used in most SQL statements, as follows:

In the SELECT list of a SELECT statement
> See the subsection "The SELECT Clause" within "Selecting Data."

In the FROM clause of a SELECT statement
> See the subsection "The FROM Clause" within "Selecting Data."

In the WHERE clause of a SELECT statement
> See "Predicates" and the subsection "The WHERE Clause" within "Selecting Data."

In the ORDER BY clause of a SELECT statement
> See the subsection "The ORDER BY Clause" within "Selecting Data."

In an INSERT...SELECT...FROM statement
> See the subsection "Subquery Inserts" within "Inserting Data."

In the SET clause of an UPDATE statement
> See the subsection "New Values from a Subquery" within "Updating Data."

A subquery in the FROM clause of a SELECT statement functions like a view, and takes the place of a table as a data source. Just as you can use views as targets of INSERT, DELETE, and UPDATE statements, you can also use subqueries as targets for those statements. For example:

```
DELETE
FROM (SELECT * FROM attraction
      WHERE government_owned='Y')
WHERE attraction_url IS NULL;
```

This statement deletes government-owned attractions without associated web sites.

The WITH Clause

ANSI/ISO defines a WITH clause that you can use to factor out a subquery so that you don't need to repeat it in your SELECT statement. Oracle and DB2 support WITH, but SQL Server and MySQL do not.

The following SELECT repeats the same subquery twice in order to generate a list of cities having more than the average number of attractions:

```
SELECT a1.city_id, COUNT(*) att_count,
       (SELECT AVG(attraction_count)
         FROM (SELECT a2.city_id,
               COUNT(*) attraction_count
               FROM attraction a2
               GROUP BY a2.city_id)) avg_att_count
FROM attraction a1
GROUP BY a1.city_id
HAVING COUNT(*) > (
SELECT AVG(attraction_count)
FROM (SELECT a2.city_id, COUNT(*) attraction_count
      FROM attraction a2
      GROUP BY a2.city_id));
```

Aside from being difficult to read and comprehend, this query is a potential maintenance disaster, as any change to the subquery needs to be made twice. Using WITH, you can rewrite the query in a way that specifies the subquery only once. The following example works for Oracle:

```
WITH average_attraction_count AS
     (SELECT
        AVG(attraction_count) avg_att_count
        FROM (SELECT a2.city_id,
              COUNT(*) attraction_count
        FROM attraction a2
        GROUP BY a2.city_id))
SELECT a1.city_id, COUNT(*) att_count,
       (SELECT avg_att_count
        FROM average_attraction_count)
FROM attraction a1
GROUP BY a1.city_id
HAVING COUNT(*) > (SELECT avg_att_count
        FROM average_attraction_count);
```

DB2 differs slightly from Oracle in how you name the columns returned by the WITH clause's query. In Oracle, you specify column aliases to name the columns. In DB2, you name the columns in parentheses following the subquery name:

```
WITH average_attraction_count
     (avg_att_count) AS
   ...
```

As you can see, the WITH clause doesn't get rid of multiple subqueries entirely, but it does allow you to place all the complex logic into the factored-out subquery, leaving only simple SELECTs for the subqueries in the main statement.

See "Hierarchical Queries" to learn how WITH is used in DB2 to write recursive queries.

WITH with Correlated Subqueries

Using WITH to factor out a non-correlated subquery, as demonstrated in the preceding section, is relatively easy. Factoring out a correlated subquery requires more thought because WITH subqueries cannot be correlated. Consider the following query, which uses a correlated subquery to return the county name for each attraction:

```
SELECT attraction_name,
       (SELECT county_name
        FROM county ct JOIN city c
          ON ct.county_id = c.county_id
        WHERE c.city_id = a.city_id)
FROM attraction a
WHERE (SELECT county_name
       FROM county ct JOIN city c
         ON ct.county_id = c.county_id
       WHERE c.city_id = a.city_id) = 'Houghton';
```

One way to rewrite this query using WITH is to place the join in the WITH subquery, but leave the correlation in the two subqueries in the main SELECT:

```
WITH silly_subquery AS
    (SELECT city_id, county_name
     FROM county ct JOIN city c
     ON ct.county_id = c.county_id)
SELECT attraction_name,
       (SELECT county_name
        FROM silly_subquery ss
        WHERE a.city_id = ss.city_id)
FROM attraction a
WHERE (SELECT county_name
       FROM silly_subquery ss
       WHERE a.city_id = ss.city_id) = 'Houghton';
```

This really doesn't buy you much, as the two subqueries in the main SELECT are merely one line shorter than before. Another approach is to join the subquery to the attraction table in the main SELECT:

```
WITH silly_subquery AS
    (SELECT city_id, county_name
     FROM county ct JOIN city c
     ON ct.county_id = c.county_id)
SELECT a.attraction_name, ss.county_name
FROM attraction a JOIN silly_subquery ss
    ON a.city_id = ss.city_id
WHERE ss.county_name = 'Houghton';
```

This is much better. Of course, if you were going to do a join, you'd have written the subquery in the FROM clause to begin with:

```
SELECT a.attraction_name, ss.county_name
FROM attraction a JOIN
    (SELECT city_id, county_name
     FROM county ct JOIN city c
        ON ct.county_id = c.county_id) ss
    ON a.city_id = ss.city_id
WHERE ss.county_name = 'Houghton';
```

This isn't to say that WITH doesn't have its place, but sometimes you're almost better off not using it. In this case, the logic in the main SELECT is probably clearer from having the subquery listed earlier, in the WITH clause. The benefit to using WITH in this instance is one of readability.

In DB2, you specify column names in the WITH clause as follows:

```
WITH silly_subquery
    (city_id, county_name)
    AS (SELECT ... )
```

In Oracle, you use column aliases, as shown in this section's examples.

Transaction Management

A *transaction* is a collection of operations treated as a unit. Either all operations in the unit are completed, or none of them are. All databases in common use make provision for transactions (although MySQL is late to the game with transaction support).

When working in a transactional environment, you need to know how to begin and end a transaction. You also need to know how to specify various characteristics of a transaction—for example, whether it will update any data.

Autocommit Mode

SQL Server and MySQL default to an autocommit mode in which each statement you execute is treated as a transaction in and of itself.

You can disable autocommit in SQL Server with the following command:

```
SET IMPLICIT_TRANSACTIONS ON
```

You can enable autocommit again using:

```
SET IMPLICIT_TRANSACTIONS OFF
```

You leave SQL Server's autocommit mode whenever you issue an explicit BEGIN TRANSACTION statement. See "Starting a Transaction" for details.

In MySQL, you can disable autocommit with:

```
SET AUTOCOMMIT=0
```

And you can enable autocommit again with:

```
SET AUTOCOMMIT=1
```

You automatically leave autocommit mode whenever you issue a BEGIN or BEGIN WORK statement.

Starting a Transaction

Databases differ in the syntax they support to begin a transaction. The following subsections show you how to begin transactions in Oracle, SQL Server, and MySQL. DB2 does not implement a SQL statement to explicitly begin a transaction.

Starting a transaction (Oracle)

With Oracle, for all practical purposes you're always in a transaction. The first SQL statement you execute after you connect implicitly begins a transaction, as does the first SQL statement you execute following the end of a transaction. Oracle's default transaction type is read-write with statement-level read consistency.

You can explicitly begin a transaction using SET TRANSACTION:

```
SET TRANSACTION options [NAME 'tran_name']

options ::=
   {READ {ONLY|WRITE}
   |ISOLATION LEVEL {SERIALIZABLE|READ COMMITTED}
   |USE ROLLBACK SEGMENT segment_name
```

The options and parameters are as follows:

NAME 'tran_name'
    Specifies a name for the transaction of up to 255 bytes. Upon COMMIT, the name will be saved as the transaction comment, overriding any COMMIT comment. It's especially helpful to name distributed transactions.

READ ONLY

Gives you a read-only transaction that does not "see" any changes committed after the transaction begins.

READ WRITE

Gives you the default transaction type: a read-write transaction with statement-level read consistency.

ISOLATION LEVEL SERIALIZABLE

Gives you a read-write, serializable transaction as defined in the SQL 1992 standard.

ISOLATION LEVEL READ COMMITTED

Gives you the default Oracle transaction behavior, but using ANSI/ISO SQL syntax.

USE ROLLBACK SEGMENT *segment_name*

Obsolete. Creates a default transaction and assigns it to the specified rollback segment. Use automatic undo management instead.

Following are some example SET TRANSACTION statements:

```
SET TRANSACTION READ ONLY;

SET TRANSACTION ISOLATION LEVEL SERIALIZABLE;

SET TRANSACTION
   ISOLATION LEVEL READ COMMITTED;
   NAME 'Delete all attractions';
```

If you name a distributed transaction and that transaction fails, your name will appear in the DBA_2PC_PENDING table's TRAN_COMMENT column.

Starting a transaction (SQL Server)

Use the following statement to explicitly begin a SQL Server transaction:

```
BEGIN TRAN[SACTION]
   [[transaction_name]
   [WITH MARK ['description']]]
```

Transaction names are limited to 32 characters. You may specify a name via a variable, as in *@variable*.

Use the WITH MARK clause to cause a transaction to be noted in the database log, optionally with a *description* that you specify.

To begin a distributed transaction, use:

```
BEGIN DISTRIBUTED TRAN[SACTION]
    [transaction_name]
```

As with BEGIN TRANSACTION, you may specify the transaction name via a variable in the form *@variable*.

SQL Server's default isolation level is READ COMMITTED. Use the following statement before beginning a transaction to specify the isolation level of your choice:

```
SET TRANSACTION ISOLATION LEVEL
    {READ COMMITTED | READ UNCOMMITTED
    |REPEATABLE READ | SERIALIZABLE}
```

This statement sets the isolation level used for all subsequent transactions in your session.

Starting a transaction (MySQL)

Use START TRANSACTION to explicitly begin a MySQL transaction (prior to MySQL 4.0.11 you'll need to use BEGIN or BEGIN WORK). When not in autocommit mode, any SQL statement you issue will implicitly begin a new transaction.

WARNING

Only certain types of MySQL tables (InnoDB tables for example) support transactions. Changes to data in non-transactional tables are made immediately and permanently, regardless of whether you are in a transaction.

Before beginning a transaction, you can use SET TRANSAC-
TION to change the transaction isolation level. A reasonable
sequence of statements might then be:

```
SET TRANSACTION ISOLATION LEVEL
    {READ UNCOMMITTED|READ COMMITTED
    |REPEATABLE READ|SERIALIZABLE};
START TRANSACTION;
```

By default, SET TRANSACTION sets the isolation level only
for your next transaction. Use SET SESSION TRANSAC-
TION to set the default isolation level for your session.

Ending a Transaction

To end a transaction and make the transaction's changes per-
manent, issue a COMMIT statement:

```
COMMIT [WORK]
```

Oracle supports an optional COMMENT clause:

```
COMMIT [WORK] [COMMENT 'text']
```

WORK is an optional word allowed by the ANSI/ISO SQL
standard (but not supported by MySQL) and is commonly
omitted. In Oracle, any name you specify using SET TRANS-
ACTION when you begin a transaction overrides any comment you may specify when you commit that transaction.

SQL Server also supports a COMMIT TRANSACTION
statement, enabling you to identify the transaction you wish
to commit:

```
COMMIT TRAN[SACTION] [transaction_name]
```

SQL Server actually ignores any transaction_name that you
specify. SQL Server allows for a name only as a convenience
to you, to make it easier for you to associate nested COM-
MITs with their corresponding BEGIN TRANSACTION
statements.

Oracle supports the following syntax to force a distributed transaction to commit:

```
COMMIT [WORK] FORCE
    {'local_tran_id'|'global_tran_id'}
    [system_change_number]
```

You identify a distributed transaction using either its local or global transaction ID, which you can obtain from the DBA_2PC_PENDING view. You have the option of assigning a system change number (SCN), or you can default to the current SCN.

Aborting a Transaction

To abort a transaction, use the ROLLBACK statement:

```
ROLLBACK [WORK]
```

As with COMMIT, the word WORK (not supported by MySQL) is commonly omitted. When you ROLLBACK a transaction, you undo all of that transaction's changes.

SQL Server also supports a ROLLBACK TRANSACTION statement, enabling you to specify the name of the transaction to roll back:

```
ROLLBACK TRAN[SACTION] [transaction_name]
```

By default, ROLLBACK TRANSACTION rolls back the current transaction. In a nested transaction, that means the innermost transaction. If you specify a transaction name, you *must* specify the outermost transaction. That transaction and all nested transactions are then undone.

Oracle supports the following syntax to force a distributed transaction to roll back:

```
ROLLBACK [WORK] FORCE
    {'local_tran_id'|'global_tran_id'}
```

You identify a distributed transaction using either its local or global transaction ID, which you can obtain from the DBA_2PC_PENDING view.

Aborting to a Transaction Savepoint

Rather than rolling back an entire transaction, you can roll back only part of a transaction. To do this, you must have marked points in the transaction, known as *savepoints*, specified using the following syntax for Oracle and MySQL:

```
SAVEPOINT savepoint_name
```

For DB2 you can specify:

```
SAVEPOINT savepoint_name [UNIQUE]
    [ON ROLLBACK RETAIN CURSORS
    [ON ROLLBACK RETAIN LOCKS]]
```

For SQL Server you can specify:

```
SAVE TRAN[SACTION] savepoint_name
```

You can then ROLLBACK to any of those savepoints using:

```
ROLLBACK [WORK] TO savepoint_name
```

Following is an example from Oracle:

```
SET TRANSACTION ISOLATION LEVEL READ COMMITTED;
UPDATE county SET state = UPPER(state);
SAVEPOINT state_upper_cased;
DELETE FROM attraction;
ROLLBACK TO state_upper_cased;
COMMIT;
```

The net effect of this transaction is to set all state abbreviations to uppercase. The DELETE against the attraction table is undone by the ROLLBACK to the savepoint established following the UPDATE statement.

Union Queries

Union queries use keywords such as UNION, EXCEPT, and INTERSECT to "combine" results from two or more queries in useful ways.

UNION and UNION ALL

Use the UNION keyword to combine results from two SELECT statements into one result set. Any duplicate rows are eliminated from the final results. Use UNION ALL to preserve duplicate rows.

UNION

The following UNION query simulates an outer join, with city being the "required" table. The first SELECT picks up cities that *can* join to the attraction table, while the second SELECT picks up those cities having no attractions:

```
SELECT c.city_name, a.attraction_name
FROM city c, attraction a
WHERE c.city_id = a.city_id
UNION
SELECT c.city_name, ''
FROM city c
WHERE c.city_id NOT IN (
    SELECT a.city_id
    FROM attraction a
    WHERE a.city_id IS NOT NULL)
ORDER BY city_name, attraction_name;
```

In DB2, you need to write the ORDER BY clause for this query as:

```
ORDER BY city_name, 2;
```

This is because DB2 does not apply the column names from the first SELECT to the entire UNION, instead generating a name in the form 1, 2, 3, etc., whenever a column name is not consistent across all queries in a UNION.

An alternative solution is to specify an alias for the computed column in the second SELECT:

```
SELECT c.city_name, '' attraction_name
```

The equivalent outer-join query is:

```
SELECT c.city_name, a.attraction_name
FROM city c LEFT OUTER JOIN attraction a
    ON c.city_id = a.city_id
ORDER BY city_name, attraction_name;
```

ANSI/SQL allows only one ORDER BY clause per query, and in a UNION query the ORDER BY clause belongs at the end. The sorting operation then applies to the collective results from all SELECT statements involved in the UNION.

UNION ALL

The following two queries demonstrate the difference between UNION and UNION ALL:

```
SELECT city_id FROM attraction
WHERE attraction_url IS NOT NULL
UNION ALL
SELECT city_id FROM attraction
WHERE government_owned='Y';

SELECT city_id FROM attraction
WHERE attraction_url IS NOT NULL
UNION
SELECT city_id FROM attraction
WHERE government_owned='Y';
```

Both queries generate a list of cities whose tourist attractions have web sites, and any city with an attraction owned by the government is listed regardless. The difference is that the UNION ALL query will list each qualifying city multiple times, whereas the UNION query eliminates duplicates, listing each qualifying city only once.

The tradeoff between UNION and UNION ALL is that UNION's duplicate elimination requires a sorting operation, which takes time because all rows must be retrieved and sorted before any results can be returned to the client who submitted the query.

Order of Evaluation

When writing a query that is the union of three or more SELECT statements, you can use parentheses to specify the order in which the union operations occur (note that MySQL does not support the use of parentheses in this manner):

```
SELECT city_id FROM city
WHERE city_name IS NULL
UNION ALL
(SELECT city_id FROM attraction
WHERE attraction_url IS NOT NULL
UNION
SELECT city_id FROM attraction
WHERE government_owned='Y');
```

Results from the second two SELECT statements are combined first, and any duplicates are eliminated because that combination represents a UNION. Next, the UNION ALL brings in any cities without names, and no duplicate elimination is performed. Thus, in this contrived example, duplicates in the results will occur for unnamed cities that have tourist attractions.

If you don't specify otherwise, union operations are performed in top-down order, except that INTERSECT takes precedence over UNION and EXCEPT.

EXCEPT (or MINUS)

Use the EXCEPT union operation (MINUS in Oracle) to "subtract" the results of one query from another. Use EXCEPT ALL when you do not desire duplicate elimination.

Neither MySQL nor SQL Server supports the EXCEPT operation.

EXCEPT

To find all cities having no attractions at all, specify:

```
SELECT city_id FROM city
EXCEPT
SELECT city_id FROM attraction;
```

This query begins with a list of all city IDs (the first SELECT), and then removes any city IDs found in the attraction table (the second SELECT).

The following query, which uses MINUS rather than EXCEPT to be compatible with Oracle, uses parentheses to specify the order of operation:

```
SELECT city_id FROM city
MINUS
(SELECT city_id FROM attraction
MINUS
SELECT city_id FROM city
WHERE city_name IS NULL);
```

Any cities with missing names are eliminated from the list of cities taken from the attraction table before that list is subtracted from the complete list of cities. Thus, cities with missing names are always included in the final results of this query.

EXCEPT ALL (DB2)

Only DB2 supports EXCEPT ALL. The following query uses that operation to return a list of cities having at least two attractions:

```
SELECT city_id FROM attraction;
EXCEPT ALL
SELECT city_id FROM city
```

The second query will return exactly one ID for each city; the first query will potentially return many IDs per city. A city with two or more attractions will have its ID listed two or more times in the results of the first query. In the case of Marquette, you end up with a subtraction that looks like this:

```
3
3
3
EXCEPT ALL
3
```

Because EXCEPT ALL was used, the single city ID from the city table is subtracted from the three from the attraction table, leaving two occurrences in the final result set:

```
3
3
```

EXCEPT ALL may not lead to the same kind of performance boost you get from using UNION ALL instead of UNION, because the EXCEPT operation still requires some sorting (or hashing) of the results in order to perform the subtraction operation.

INTERSECT

Use the INTERSECT operation to find rows in common between the result sets of two SELECTs. Use INTERSECT ALL when you do not want duplicate elimination.

Neither MySQL nor SQL Server supports the INTERSECT operation.

INTERSECT

The following INTERSECT query finds names that are used for both cities and counties:

```
SELECT city_name FROM city
INTERSECT
SELECT county_name FROM county;
```

Some kind of sorting or hashing operation will be done to find rows in common between the two result sets. Duplicate elimination ensures that each name is returned only once.

INTERSECT ALL

Use INTERSECT ALL when you want to consider duplicates. For example, given the following data:

```
MARQUETTE
MARQUETTE
BARAGA
BARAGA
MUNISING
INTERSECT ALL
MARQUETTE
MARQUETTE
BARAGA
```

INTERSECT will yield:

```
MARQUETTE
BARAGA
```

Whereas INTERSECT ALL will yield:

```
MARQUETTE
MARQUETTE
BARAGA
```

Because Marquette appears twice in both result sets, it
appears twice in the final results. Baraga, on the other hand,
appears only once in the second result set, so it appears just
once in the final result set.

Updating Data

Use the UPDATE statement to modify existing data in a
table. You can update one row or a set of rows; you can specify a single set of new values in the statement; or you can
generate new values through a subquery.

Simple Updates

A simple UPDATE takes the following form:

```
UPDATE table
SET column = value, column = value ...
WHERE predicates
```

In this form, *predicates* identify one or more rows that you want to update. You can specify as many *column = value* pairs as you like, one for each column you want to modify. For example:

```
UPDATE artist
SET website = 'outthewindow.gennick.com'
WHERE name = 'Jenny Gennick';
```

When you specify just one new value, you usually will want to update just one row, and your WHERE clause predicates should reference primary or unique key values to identify that row. Using expressions, you can write sensible UPDATEs that modify many rows:

```
UPDATE cd
SET title = UPPER(title),
    price = ROUND((price * 1.10),2);
```

This example raises the price of CDs by 10%, and also uppercases each CD title.

New Values from a Subquery

You can also generate new values from a subquery. One way to do this is to write separate subqueries for each column that you are updating:

```
UPDATE table
SET column = (subquery), column = (subquery), ...
```

For example:

```
UPDATE cd
SET total_time = (
        SELECT SUM(playing_time)
        FROM song
        WHERE song.cd_id = cd.cd_id);
```

Subqueries such as this must always be correlated, and must always return just one row and column. In this case, the subquery sums the playing_time of all the individual songs on a CD, and returns one value that is placed into the total_time column of the cd table.

You can also write a subquery that returns more than one column value, in which case the number of values returned must correspond to the columns you are updating (neither SQL Server nor MySQL support this syntax):

```
UPDATE table
SET (column, column, ...) = (subquery)
```

For example:

```
UPDATE cd
SET (first_track, artist) = (
        SELECT title, artist
        FROM song
        WHERE song.cd_id = cd.cd_id
          AND track = 1);
```

This example places the title and artist of each CD's first track into the cd table.

Updating Through a Cursor

If you're updating through a cursor, you can specify in your WHERE clause that you want to update whichever row your cursor currently points to:

```
UPDATE table
SET ...
WHERE CURRENT OF cursor_name
```

DB2 and SQL Server support this syntax, but Oracle and MySQL do not.

Updating Views and Subqueries

As with DELETE, you can specify a view or a subquery as the target of an UPDATE statement:

```
UPDATE cd_song
   SET title = INITCAP(title);
```

Neither SQL Server nor MySQL supports this syntax.

Different databases place somewhat different restrictions on this practice, but in general you must be able to unambiguously get to a single table row from a given view row in order to issue an update against that view or subquery.

Updating a Partition (Oracle)

Oracle lets you restrict updates to specific partitions and subpartitions:

```
UPDATE table PARTITION name
```

or:

```
UPDATE table SUBPARTITION name
```

Be careful about embedding the names of partitions and subpartitions into your programs, as DBAs can change partitioning over time. In some cases, Oracle's optimizer will correctly prune partitions based on the predicates you specify in your WHERE clause.

Returning the Updated Data (Oracle)

Oracle supports the following form of UPDATE, which returns information about the rows updated:

```
UPDATE ...
SET ...
WHERE ...
RETURNING expression [,expression ...]
INTO variable [,variable ...]
```

If you update a single row, Oracle expects to return values into bind variables. If you update more than one row, Oracle expects to return values into bind arrays.

UPDATE FROM Clause (SQL Server)

SQL Server lets you write a FROM clause in an UPDATE statement in order to gather columns from multiple tables for use in your SET expressions. In the earlier section "New Values from a Subquery," a subquery was used to retrieve the title and artist from the song table for each CD's first track so that those values could be stored redundantly in their corresponding cd row. In SQL Server, you can accomplish the same feat using the FROM clause:

```
UPDATE cd
    SET first_track = song.title,
        artist = song.artist
FROM cd INNER JOIN song
    ON cd.cd_id = song.cd_id
WHERE song.track = 1;
```

When using this syntax, ensure that the UPDATE is *deterministic*, i.e., that there is only one possible value for any column you reference in a SET expression. The WHERE clause in this example ensures that song.title and song.artist refer to only one combination of title and artist from the song table. Without that WHERE clause, there would be as many song/title combinations per CD as tracks on that CD. In such a many-to-one case, the statement may succeed, but there's no rule controlling which of those song/title combinations would be used.

If you reference the updated table more than once in the FROM clause, all but one of those references must be given table aliases.

Index

Symbols

* (asterisk) regular-expression
  metacharacter, 104, 106
  COUNT function and, 57
  qualifying with table
    names, 108
  returning all columns from a
    table, 107
= and =, designating left and right
  outer joins, 87
^ (caret) regular-expression
  metacharacter, 104, 105
^= comparison operator, 97
$ (dollar sign) regular-expression
  metacharacter, 104, 106
(\) escape character, 101, 104
  MySQL regular expressions
    and, 105
? (question mark) regular-
  expression
  metacharacter, 104, 106
% (percent), used for pattern
  matching, 100, 105
. (period), used for pattern
  matching, 100, 104, 105
| (pipe) regular-expression
  metacharacter, 104, 106
+ (plus) regular-expression
  metacharacter, 104, 106
  identifying optional tables, 87
  string concatenation
    operator, 53

|| string concatenation
  operator, 53
_ (underscore), used for pattern
  matching, 101, 105
!= comparison operator, 97
< comparison operator, 97
< > comparison operator, 97
<= comparison operator, 97, 100
<=> comparison operator, 97
= comparison operator, 97, 119
> comparison operator, 97
>= comparison operator, 97, 100
(...) regular-expression
  metacharacters, 104, 106
[...] regular-expression
  metacharacters, 104, 105
[[.xx.]] regular-expression
  metacharacters, 106
[[:<:]] regular-expression
  metacharacters, 106
[[:>:]] regular-expression
  metacharacters, 106
[.xx.] regular-expression
  metacharacters, 104
[:class:] regular-expression
  metacharacters, 104, 106
[=chars=] regular-expression
  metacharacters, 104, 106
[^ ...] regular-expression
  metacharacters, 104, 105
\1 ... \9 regular-expression
  metacharacters, 104
{x}, {x,y}, {x,} regular-expression
  metacharacters, 104, 106

We'd like to hear your suggestions for improving our indexes. Send email to
index@oreilly.com.

regexes (see regular expressions)
REGEXP predicate, 97, 105
REGEXP_INSTR function, 51, 102
REGEXP_LIKE function, 97, 102
REGEXP_REPLACE function, 52, 102
REGEXP_SUBSTR function, 52, 102
regular expressions, 102–106
    metacharacters, 104–106
    MySQL, 105
    Oracle, 102–104
    SQL Server, 104
REMAINDER function, 49
REPLACE function, 52
required tables in outer
        joins, 84–87
result sets, 106
    column names
        controlling, 110
        specifying, 107
    combining, using UNION
        keyword, 132
    duplicate rows, eliminating, 114
    finding rows in common, using
        INTERSECT, 136
RETURNING clause
    deleted data, returned by, 38
    inserted values, returned by, 75
    updated data, returned by, 140
right outer joins, 85
RLIKE comparison operator, 97
ROLLBACK statement
    aborting to transaction
        savepoints, 131
    aborting transactions, 130
    deleting data and, 35
    warning about TRUNCATE
        statement and, 36
ROLLBACK TRANSACTION
        statement, 130
ROLLUP operation
    Oracle, 61
    SQL Server, 64
ROUND function, 44, 49
rows
    deleting from tables, 35
    eliminating duplicates, 115
    EXISTS/NOT EXISTS
        predicates, 99
    filtering, using HAVING, 60

grouping into sets, 56–61
inserting into tables, 72–76
INTERSECT operation, 136
joining tables, 77–87
loops in hierarchical data, 70
MERGE statement, 91
retrieving all, 114
returning information about
        deleted rows, 38
summarizing data, 61–65
TRUNCATE TABLE vs.
        DELETE, 36
UNION/UNION ALL
        keywords, 132
updating data, 137–141
WHERE clause, 119
RTRIM function, 54

S

savepoints, aborting to, 131
scalar functions, 41–56
schema names, qualifying table
        names by, 114
SCNs (system change
        numbers), 40
searched CASE expressions, 8
searching strings, functions for, 51
SEC_TO_TIME function, 31
SECOND function, 18, 29
SECOND keyword (MySQL), 47
seconds since 1-Jan-1970,
        converting datetimes
        into, 31
seconds-of-the-day, converting
        datetimes into, 31
SELECT statement, 106–120
    column names in result sets
        controlling, 110
        specifying, 107
    embedding subqueries in, 113
    expressions, using in, 109
    FROM clause and, 116–119
    GROUP BY queries and, 59
    ORDER BY clause, 120
    recursive WITH clause and, 66
    using subqueries in, 121–124
    subquery inserts in, 74
    union queries and, 132–137
    WHERE clause and, 119